Parental Involvement and Peer Tutoring in Mathematics and Science

Developing Paired Maths
into Paired Science

Keith Topping and Judi Bamford

with Tiny Arora, Anne Mallinson
and Kay Shanahan

David Fulton Publishers

David Fulton Publishers Ltd
Ormond House, 26–27 Boswell Street, London WC1N 3JD

First published in Great Britain by David Fulton Publishers 1998

British Library Cataloguing in Publication Data
A catalogue record for this book is available from the British Library

ISBN 1–85346–541–0

Typeset by Textype Typesetters, Cambridge
Printed in Great Britain by The Cromwell Press Ltd, Trowbridge, Wiltshire

Contents

Preface   v

1   Introduction, rationale and development   1

2   Materials: selecting and creating maths games   20

3   Organising parental involvement in maths and science   31

4   Research findings in Paired Maths and Science   44

5   How to evaluate Paired Maths and Science   62

6   Cooperative learning and peer tutoring in the maths classroom   71

7   Cross-school peer tutoring in maths for special needs   83

8   Conclusions and future directions   89

Appendices – Further information and resources   94

1   Details of Paired Maths project games: Levels 1, 2 and 3   94

2   List of suppliers of games and other useful addresses   100

3   List of games and puzzle books   101

4   List of software suppliers   104

5   List of websites   104

6   Parents' mathematical library – bibliography   106

7   Further reading for professionals   107

References   108

Subject and author index   115

Preface

Paired Maths is a system for parents, peers and other non-professional tutors to interact with children using selected structured mathematical games (unlike ordinary schoolwork or 'games' from commercial maths schemes), with the aim of consolidating and deepening maths understanding and generalising problem solving skills out of the classroom into 'real-life' community settings, as well as increasing enjoyment, motivation and confidence in all partners.

Paired Science is a parallel system for science, except instead of 'games' the interaction is guided by a series of 'Activity Sheets'. These outline suggested activities, list the simple materials needed, and give instructions for children and advice for helpers.

This book is one of a family of three related books, consisting of two resource Handbooks for everyday use, supported by a more detailed background text for deeper reading and reference.

The three Paired Maths and Science books

The Paired Maths Handbook (by Keith Topping and Judi Bamford) gives a brief introduction to the rationale, materials, organisation and evaluation of the Paired Maths method for parental involvement and peer tutoring in mathematics, for children aged 4 to 14. This is followed by twelve different practical resources to copy to help with the organisation of the method. The main part of the book consists of two-dimensional mathematical games to copy, complete with instructions and needing minimal other materials. These games are particularly suitable for children aged 9 to 12, especially when involved in cooperative learning or peer tutoring in schools or other study centres (although they can also be used in parental involvement, and with older children with difficulties with maths).

The Paired Science Handbook (by Keith Topping) gives a brief introduction to the rationale, history, materials, organisation and evaluation of the Paired Science method for parental involvement and peer tutoring in science. This is followed by eight different resources to copy to help with organisation. The main part consists of Paired Science Activity Sheets to copy, complete with instructions for children and helpers, and needing little equipment other than that already available in most homes and schools. These activity sheets are particularly suitable for children aged 5 to 7, especially when engaged in parental involvement projects linking home and school, (although they can also be used in cross-age peer tutoring in schools or other study centres up to the age of 11, and with older children with difficulties with science).

The more detailed background text (by Keith Topping and Judi Bamford) is titled 'Parental Involvement and Peer Tutoring in Mathematics and Science'. Its subtitle 'Developing Paired Maths into Paired Science' indicates that its main focus is the Paired Maths method, which has a longer history and wider research than the more recent Paired Science work. However, much of the rationale and many of the organisational issues and possible applications are common to both, and the implications for Paired Science are also explored throughout the book. Coordinators of parent involvement or peer tutoring projects and maths and science specialists or coordinators will find the practical guidance in this book about materials, organisation and evaluation essential reading. More information is also included about related international developments and research findings, and extension of the methods to more challenging target groups. This, of course, is the book you are now reading.

Structure of this book

The first chapter discusses changes in thinking about mathematics education and the cyclic concerns about falling standards in comparison to other countries and gender bias within countries. It then describes the origins of the Paired Maths method using mathematical games, as a development from Paired Reading. The psycho-educational theory underpinning Paired Maths is briefly reviewed. Differences from other approaches, such as 'Family Math' and the 'IMPACT' programme, are highlighted, and the advantages of the Paired Maths approach described. The implications for the development of Paired Science are then reviewed.

Chapter 2 explores the requirements for successful games and outlines the different categorical structures used at the three National Curriculum levels. The mathematical rationale for the games and the mathematical subskills they aim to develop are outlined. Various means of acquiring and/or producing a 'kit' of games are discussed. Materials for the development of Paired Science are then reviewed.

Key issues in organising a Paired Maths or Science project with parental involvement are reviewed in Chapter 3, covering establishing objectives, selecting target groups, recruiting parents, selection and matching of partners, organising access to games, controlling experience of various areas of mathematics, setting up a training or 'launch' meeting, establishing time scales and expectations, content of the training meeting, monitoring subsequent activity, trouble-shooting, feedback of evaluation results and keeping the momentum and novelty going.

Chapter 4 considers research findings on the effectiveness of Paired Maths, both from the wider background literature on related methods and from the research undertaken by the authors specifically on Paired Maths parental involvement projects. Reference is made to research findings on Paired Science.

Different ways of evaluating your own Paired Maths or Paired Science project are described in Chapter 5, including formative process evaluation, group discussions, individual feedback questionnaires, standardised mathematics tests, curriculum-based assessments and attitudinal and motivational measures. Evaluation methods specific to Paired Science are then considered.

Chapter 6 describes the organisation, operation and evaluation of Paired Maths on a class-wide basis through cooperative learning and peer tutoring between children within the primary classroom, giving practical guidelines and recommendations to ensure success and detailed research results.

Peer tutored Paired Maths occurring between pupils from a primary school and a special school, alternately in each location, is described in Chapter 7. The viability of the approach with children with severe learning difficulties is discussed, as are the gains accruing to pupils from both establishments. Chapters 6 and 7 both have implications for extension into Paired Science.

The concluding chapter briefly summarises the state of the art and discusses possible future developments and research, including increasing access to cooperative mathematical and science activities in the home via the Internet.

The Appendices (1–7) include further details on maths games used at different levels, further information on game suppliers, other books of games, software suppliers, and Internet websites, with suggestions for stocking a parents' mathematical library and other further reading.

Audience for the book

This book is directed principally at teachers and those who train, support and manage teachers. Some members of the research community will also find interest in the book. Some parents might find interest in the book, but many are likely to find the more immediately practical accompanying 'Handbooks' more appealing.

It seeks to give readers sufficient organisational detail to enable them not only to replicate but also creatively extend the Paired Maths and Paired Science approaches successfully, whether through parental or peer involvement, with primary or secondary aged children, with 'ordinary' children or those with special needs. Relevant background theory and effectiveness research are reviewed in an accessible way leading directly to implications for action.

Contributors

Much of the earlier work on parental involvement in mathematics was greatly enhanced by the input of Tiny Arora, who is currently Associate Tutor to the postgraduate professional training course in educational psychology at the University of Sheffield and Senior Educational Psychologist in the Kirklees Education Support Service in West Yorkshire. Chapter 6 on Cooperative Learning and Peer Tutoring in the classroom is largely based on the work of Anne Mallinson, who is an Educational Psychologist with the Stirling Psychological Service in Scotland. Chapter 7 on cross-school peer tutoring for special needs is largely based on the work of Kay Shanahan, who is the In-service Training Coordinator and a class teacher at Highfields Special School in Huddersfield, West Yorkshire.

How to use the book

The introductory chapter (1) is best read first, but is quite substantial. If you are not inclined to read all of it in sequence, the first paragraph and the last three sections (The Objectives, History and Development of Paired Maths; Why Paired Maths is Different; Implications for Paired Science) are crucial. After that, the consecutive middle sections on The Language of Maths, Maths Games, Cooperative Learning in Maths and Science, Peer Tutoring in Maths and Science and Parental Involvement in Maths Internationally are probably the most important. Readers are recommended then to read Chapters 2 and 3, in that order. Thereafter, the reader should have enough background to be able to dabble according to interest without confusion.

Keith Topping
Judi Bamford
January 1998

Bibliography

Topping, K. J. (1995) *Paired Reading, Spelling and Writing: The Handbook for Teachers and Parents.* London & New York: Cassell.

Topping, K. J. (1998) *The Paired Science Handbook: Parental Involvement and Peer Tutoring in Science.* London: David Fulton Publishers; Bristol PA: Taylor & Francis.

Topping, K. J. and Bamford, J. (1998) *The Paired Maths Handbook: Parental Involvement and Peer Tutoring in Mathematics.* London: David Fulton Publishers; Bristol PA: Taylor & Francis.

Topping, K. J. and Bamford, J. (1998) *Parental Involvement and Peer Tutoring in Mathematics and Science: Developing Paired Maths into Paired Science.* London: David Fulton Publishers; Bristol PA: Taylor & Francis.

CHAPTER 1

Introduction, rationale and development

Welcome! This chapter begins by considering the cyclic concerns about falling standards in mathematics compared with other countries. These concerns constantly recur, and need to be addressed in the context of the uneasy relationship which exists between 'school' maths and science and the demands of everyday life and of particular vocations. The problem of the transmission of negative attitudes to mathematics and science from one generation to another is reviewed, with particular reference to gender differences. Changes in thinking about mathematics education are discussed and the significance of language in learning and understanding maths emphasised.

As part of these changes, the role and functional impact of mathematical games and cooperative learning and peer tutoring in maths and science are examined. International work on parental involvement in maths is related to similar work in the UK. This leads into a discussion of the objectives, provenance, history and development of the Paired Maths approach presented in this book. Differences from other approaches are highlighted, and the positive advantages of the Paired Maths approach described. Finally, the specific implications for the development of Paired Science are outlined.

The usefulness and importance of maths

Numeracy matters. Poor numeracy skills are a major disadvantage in everyday life and in the job market. The National Child Development Study found that 25 per cent of adults aged 37 had numeracy skills so low as to make it difficult to complete everyday tasks such as shopping successfully (Bynner and Parsons 1997). Men with poor numeracy skills were more prone to unemployment, more likely to be in manual jobs, less likely to have had work-related training and more likely to earn a low weekly wage. Restricted numeracy also had some impact on women, who were more likely to be in part time jobs: only 25 per cent with poor numeracy held a full-time job compared to 40 per cent of those with adequate numeracy. Alarmingly, less than 20 per cent of those with poor numeracy skills as adults were identified as poor at maths by their teachers. Furthermore, there was evidence that adequate literacy had little effect in cushioning the impact of poor numeracy in adult life.

However, it cannot be assumed that more teaching in school would solve the problem, since there is also concern about the relationship between the school mathematics curriculum (before and after the National Curriculum) and the mathematical demands of everyday life and employment. A survey by Raines (1988) indicated parents were frequently critical of the relevance of the school mathematics they had learned to later life. As Nunes *et al.* (1993) point out in their exploration of the relationship between school mathematics and street mathematics, children can carry out quite complex arithmetical calculations in relation to their life needs without any formal teaching, while subsequently proving unable to do equivalent problems in school, where the problem is not only decontextualised but a different and singular route to the solution is required. There is not only a lack of generalisation of school mathematics to real life, there is a lack of generalisation of the mathematics of real life to the school.

The Cockcroft Report (1982) was an important landmark for mathematics education in the UK and recognised and emphasised the importance of parental influence and the early age by which attitudes to mathematics are fixed. It defined the aims of mathematics teaching as developing powers of logical thought and equipping children with numerical skills. The research for the Cockcroft Report suggested that after three years in secondary (high) school, children understood important mathematical concepts very little better than when they left primary (elementary) school, sometimes less well. More recently the National Curriculum assessment has suggested that a range as wide as seven years could be expected in the mathematical attainments of children at the beginning of their secondary education.

Standards in mathematics internationally

Over the years considerable concern has been expressed about the performance of children in the UK in mathematics at primary and secondary level when compared to the performance of children from other countries.

The report *Learning Mathematics and Science: The Second International Assessment of Educational Progress in England* (Foxman 1992) involved 20 countries in examining the attainment of 9- and 13-year-olds in maths and science (some countries only examined attainments at age 13). The results did not make reassuring reading. Pupils from England and Wales and the USA performed poorly in mathematics and science relative to pupils from other countries. Switzerland achieved the best results at age 13 in Europe, while pupils from Korea outperformed those from the other countries.

The Third International Mathematics and Science Study (TIMMS) (e.g. Scottish Office 1996a) involved 40 participating countries in 1995. In the first two years of high school, Singapore, Korea, Japan and Hong Kong occupied the first four places. England, Scotland and the USA hovered around 20th place, below a number of Eastern European countries where children had experienced a year less in school. Scotland was characterised by relatively high numbers of hours devoted to mathematics teaching and high availability of remedial mathematics teaching, but low use of homework, high use of calculators, high use of worksheets and textbooks, and a greater tendency to blame poor results on low pupil ability.

A study of mathematics ability in adulthood in seven industrialised countries left Britain bottom of the list (Basic Skills Agency 1997). Japan was top. Women did worse than men. Subjects were aged 16 to 60, and the older subjects did better than the younger.

Caution is needed in the interpretation of these results. Such 'league tables' often mask quite small absolute differences between countries, different outcomes at different ages and stages, and different distributions of scores between different countries (e.g. in 1991, able British mathematicians did as well as Koreans, but low-attaining pupils did much worse). Nevertheless, there was little ground here for complacency.

The Scottish Office (1996b) *Assessment of Achievement Programme: Mathematics 1994* survey of maths in Scottish schools examined performance at Primary 4 (P4, age 8), Primary 7 (P7, age 11) and Secondary 2 (age 13) levels in mathematics, relating them to the Scottish 5–14 Curriculum (Scotland does not have the same mandatory 'National Curriculum' as England and Wales and chronological year bands have different labels). The apparent drop in mathematics performance in several areas from 1991 to 1994 provoked widespread concern, as did the developing trend for mathematics performance to decline as children grew older. In problem-solving some pupils often used a random approach rather than a systematic one. Consequently, more emphasis was subsequently placed on solving a wider range of problems in context with direct teaching of strategies coupled with more practical experience and group discussion.

Attitudes to maths

For children with learning difficulties, the hierarchical nature of mathematics as a subject of study has often meant 'going back to basics' – repeating what has already not been understood but with the effect of facing failure yet again – with the result that, as the Cockcroft Report (1982) observed: 'by the end of the primary years a child's attitude to mathematics is often becoming fixed . . . and for many this meant being fixed as an attitude of rejection and antagonism'.

The survey by Raines (1988) showed that mathematics was an emotive topic for parents – even in middle-class areas and schools with good home–school relations. Enjoyment of mathematics and self-concept were closely linked; very few parents who saw themselves as good at mathematics disliked doing it, whilst most of the parents who saw themselves as bad at mathematics hated it, especially at secondary school. The latter parents had strong memories of school experiences, often unfavourable. Many parents felt the aims of mathematics teaching in schools should include the development of confidence and enthusiasm as well as understanding. These findings led Raines to criticise 'parental involvement in maths' schemes which were merely 'shipping home the curriculum' as naïvely ignoring the affective and historical dimensions of parents' own reality.

Disliking mathematics can all too readily be construed as 'normal'. Adults seem prepared to say 'I'm no good at maths' or 'I never was any good at maths at school' when they are very unlikely to be as ready to say 'I can't read'. Askew and Wiliam (1995) found that 'pupils' self confidence and beliefs affect their success in mathematics', and argued that those who lacked confidence in their ability try to avoid challenges and show little persistence. The danger of parents' modelling negative attitudes to mathematics which are then adopted by children and become a self-fulfilling prophecy is apparent.

Any attempt to involve parents in a more active role in mathematical education thus needs to make allowance for the influence of past experiences on their self-image and confidence. The work reported in this book was deliberately designed to deal with this, through inviting the parents to a pre-project meeting initially without their children. This gave them the opportunity to play, learn and rehearse the games without embarrassment, provided both positive reinforcement and enthusiastic modelling and offered positive practice with non-threatening feedback. They also openly discussed misconceptions about their own everyday use of, and effectiveness with, mathematical knowledge, and finally considered how their own attitude to mathematics might affect their children's learning.

Gender differentials

Differences between girls' and boys' attainment in mathematics has been the focus of debate and concern for many years. However, the research evidence does not always substantiate popular assumptions.

For instance, Askew and Wiliam (1995) found that up to age 11 the achievement of girls and boys was comparable, while at age 15 boys scored higher than girls across mathematics topics, although the latter tendency was decreasing. In the TIMMS study mentioned earlier (Scottish Office 1996a) boys performed better than girls in 31 out of 38 countries in the early years of secondary school, but the difference was only statistically significant in six. As in previous studies, differences between countries were certainly greater than differences between genders (cf. Hanna 1989).

The Assessment of Achievement Programme (Scottish Office 1996b) survey suggested little general difference in the performance of girls and boys on most tasks carried out in their survey. However, it was reported that girls outperformed boys in a 'minority of tasks' at P4 (Year 3, eight-year-olds); while boys did better than girls at P7 (Year 6, eleven-year-olds), again yielding some evidence of a relative gender decline over the years.

This echoed some earlier research from the USA, which had suggested that girls' interest and confidence in mathematics dropped in early adolescence before their actual performance in maths dropped (Fennema and Sherman 1978, Fennema and Meyer 1989). This led to the proposal that if their interest and confidence could be maintained, so could their performance. In the USA a number of programmes aiming to achieve this have been established (Campbell 1995), such as 'Eureka' and 'Operation

Smart'. The important common elements seem to be: many hands-on activities, inbuilt enjoyment, providing time for questions, relaxed activities with little or no emphasis on individual competition, and many opportunities to see that mathematics and science are as readily 'girl' fields as boys'.

Leder (1990) noted that in the mathematics classroom, boys interacted more frequently than girls with their teachers, both seeking and receiving more attention. The girls' lower frequency of interaction might be connected to their loss of interest and confidence and the subsequent falling off of their performance in mathematics, although the causal direction is difficult to establish.

Other international studies of gender differences in maths attainment have produced mixed results. Many have found no gender differences (e.g. Stocking and Goldstein 1992 with high ability secondary students, Sedlacek 1990 at third grade level, Kohr *et al.* 1989 at fifth, eight and eleventh grade, and Tartre and Fennema 1995 at any grade 6–12 in a longitudinal study). Some of these have found race and socio-economic differences to have greater impact (e.g. Kohr *et al.* 1989, Sedlacek 1990).

Some have found gender differences favouring males which were however small (e.g. the Hyde *et al.* 1990 meta-analysis of mathematical attitudes and affect, and Manger's (1995) study of Norwegian third graders – although in the latter there were more marked gender differences at the extreme tails of the distribution). Few studies have found differences reaching statistical significance, although Brown's (1991) study did so, finding second and fifth grade girls better than boys at reading while the boys were ahead in mathematics achievement. However, Brandon *et al.* (1987) found girls in Hawaii did better than boys in grades four, six, eight and ten.

Teachers and peers are of course not the only potential source of any gender stereotyping regarding mathematics. Children's beliefs about their own achievement seem related more to parental expectation about the child's achievement than to the parents' own level of achievement. There has been particular interest in maternal expectations of daughter's achievement in mathematics, but significant effects found only with more highly educated mothers and/or high achieving daughters (Jayaratne 1987, Dickens and Cornell 1990).

In summary, gender differences in mathematics achievement might be small in general and reducing, but they might nevertheless be educationally significant at later ages, at certain ability levels, in certain countries and cultural groups, and in certain mathematical topics. However, the transmission of negative gender stereotyping in relation to achievement expectations is clearly undesirable from any source, and enhancing parental encouragement in this regard would seem a useful component of any project.

Learning maths

The teaching and learning of mathematics has been strongly influenced over the years by various contributions from different psychologists and educationalists.

Piaget's stage theory of the child's cognitive development in mathematics was detailed in *The Child's Conception of Number* (1952). Children were thought to progress inevitably through stages: Sensori-motor (birth to 2 years), Pre-operational (2–7 years), Concrete Operational (7–11 years) and Formal Operational (11+ years). Piaget's stage theory and concepts about thinking processes such as equilibration, assimilation and accommodation were widely adopted by educators and applied to the classroom. Piagetian educators believed that the child must pass through each stage before becoming ready to move on to a higher one, that the child could not be taught to function at a higher level until 'ready' for it, and that the child was an active constructor of his or her own knowledge through interaction with materials.

Although Piaget's (1952) emphasis on the need for mathematics to be embodied in concrete activities before conventional symbolism can be utilised was important, there have since been several re-interpretations of Piaget's theory, suggesting that parts of it were flawed (e.g. Gelman and Gallistel 1978, Brainerd 1978, Donaldson 1978, Bower 1981, Light 1986, Wood 1988). Criticisms focused on over-rigid interpretation of the stages and their sequential inevitability, and the related notion of 'readiness'. Piaget was accused of neglecting the effects of linguistic and cultural contexts and discontinuities in these between home and school. It was suggested that concepts such as conservation were actually largely historically and culturally determined.

Concerning collaborative learning, Piaget's view was that this would optimally occur in groups of children of similar ability in mathematics, but with different interpretations and strategies for problem-solving. The 'cognitive conflict' resulting from the ensuing debate among equals stimulated rethinking by all group members and led to new assimilations and accommodations. However, the implication that mathematics could best be learnt by discovery and argument was strongly challenged by proponents of direct instruction, not least on the grounds of cost effectiveness.

An alternative view of learning was proposed by Vygotsky, whose most well-known books are probably *Thought and Language* (1962) and *Mind in Society* (1978). Vygotsky believed learning was socially, culturally and historically determined. He saw language as a vital instrument to regulate behaviour and organise thinking, thus creating new perceptions, memories and thought processes. Vygotsky viewed children as active agents in the educational process, but disagreed that 'readiness' or maturity was necessary for learning. On the contrary, teaching created learning and learning led development, in a complex and dynamic relationship.

Almost all learning was in a sense collaborative, typically through interaction between a more expert agent and a novice. Collaboration between children was best arranged on a cross-ability basis, so that higher order mental processes valued in the host culture could be modelled and transmitted through a form of 'apprenticeship'. The teacher or more expert partner offered the learner structured prompts or 'scaffolding' to enable them to learn by supported functioning at a higher level (within their 'zone of proximal development') than they could have managed independently.

Within the Paired Maths framework using mathematical games described in this book, collaborative learning through both the Piagetian and Vygotskian models is likely to occur. Cognitive conflict is promoted through the requirements for competition in many games, and the element of random chance often makes adult and child effectively equals. However, particularly when a new player is introduced to a game, much prompting and scaffolding by more experienced players is required. In either event the participants are motivated to achieve their own self-selected (and therefore presumably culturally acceptable) purposes. However, the participants continuously determine the current level of cognitive challenge for themselves during the process of learning, rather than having it prescribed by an outsider. Equally, in either event, a great deal of discussion and debate of the inherent mathematical procedures and processes often ensues and is to be encouraged. As Hughes (1986) argued, the provision of concrete experiences alone is insufficient – the goal is to help enhance children's thinking so that they can understand, express and generalise mathematical concepts, using language and symbolism as necessary.

An emphasis on the importance of culturally transmitted knowledge was also evident in Jerome Bruner's writing on education and instruction (1960, 1966, 1971), which was influenced by Vygotsky. Bruner believed that learning involved searching and discovery through physical and visual experiences and the use of practical apparatus, the internalisation of a model of the world selectively derived from experience but going beyond it, and the use of language and symbols to order that model. However, systematic instruction could and should facilitate and speed discovery. He rejected the stages of development, asserting that a child could in principle be taught any subject at any stage (1960), including mathematical games with rules derived from advanced mathematics.

Skemp (1971, 1978, 1989a) suggested many mathematics learners were insecure in their understanding and therefore relied on habit-learning, rather than developing generalisable concepts or models. He defined habit-learning as being concerned with getting particular results, giving the right answers to a limited class of questions, in effect 'tricks for ticks' – with very little encouragement to relate these recipes to concrete experience. Skemp was concerned about an excess of direct instruction in which the teacher modelled the conventional method, which the pupils then sought to imitate. For Skemp, the essence of intelligent learning was adaptability – being able to learn from encounters with the physical world, matching experience against expectation, communicating with and learning from others and comparing ideas with them, and being able to develop and build mathematical models which yielded creative and testable predictions.

The approach recommended by Skemp was activity- and game-based, with an emphasis on discussion and cooperation. Similarly, Whitebread (1995) proposed four key areas in the teaching of mathematics: starting with real problems in meaningful contexts, encouraging children to represent their mathematical understanding verbally and graphically, encouraging children to develop their own mathematical strategies and involving children in discussing and reflecting on mathematical processes.

Relatedly, Nunes and Bryant (1996) emphasised that mathematics is a socially defined activity. Children have a great deal of early understanding of mathematical concepts, which is generative and changes during childhood, but they may perceive the mathematical demands of one social situation quite differently from those of another even where essentially the same concepts are involved, deploying their mathematical reasoning fully in one but not the other. 'School' mathematics can all too easily consist only of applications and purposes, methodologies and solutions which are socially approved within the context of the classroom by the dominant cultural influence – the teacher. The result of the discontinuity between the classroom and 'real life' can be that the child's conception of what mathematics *is* narrows – and the child can be disempowered.

In attempting to start from the child's own point of departure in terms of understanding, the role of discussion is widely seen as crucial. In a subject as abstract as mathematics it is essential that children's verbal comprehension and expression of mathematics are carefully monitored, thereby giving a more effective window onto deeper understanding than correct outcomes of computations, and enabling misconceptions to be tackled as soon as possible. However, children may be reluctant to engage in mathematical 'think alouds' with their teacher for fear of being wrong and feeling foolish. Paired Maths activities with peers enable a lower threshold of self-disclosure and give the teacher the opportunity to circulate to diagnose misconceptions by strategic overhearing. Something similar might be true for some parents at home.

The value of peer-assisted learning in helping diagnose misconceptions is also emphasised by Topping and Ehly (1998), who list other possible factors which might account for the success of Paired Maths (and indeed Paired Science).

Cognitively, these include increases (for helpers, helped, or both) in:

- attention,
- time on task and engagement,
- positive practice,
- fluency – speed of response,
- modelling which is proximate and credible,
- prompting,
- immediacy and timeliness of tutor intervention,
- individualisation of learning,
- individual accountability and responsibility,
- planning and rehearsal,
- cognitive restructuring through new associations and integrations,
- explaining with exemplification and analogising – in vernacular language,
- questioning – intelligently and adaptively,
- predicting and estimating,
- the modulation of information processing – preventing overload,
- responding opportunities,
- identification of gaps and engineering closure,
- error opportunities leading to error identification and analysis and self-correction opportunities,
- feedback opportunities,
- reinforcement, and
- self-assessment and self-regulation.

Affectively, these might include:

- variety and interest,
- activity and inter-activity,
- modelling of enthusiasm and coping,
- identification and bonding,
- ownership of the learning process, and
- self-confidence, self-belief and self-efficacy.

Whichever combination of these factors are at play in any one Paired Maths interaction, all the 'experts' agree that the role of language is crucial.

The language of maths

Four essential components of children 'doing mathematics' were suggested by Jones and Haylock (1985): concrete experience involving motor activity, language, pictures and symbols. As we have noted earlier, children and their parents and teachers talk and listen mathematics as well as visualise, read and write it, and discussion is crucial in developing understanding, especially for children with learning difficulties in this area (Daniels and Anghileri 1995).

As with other curricular areas (e.g. science), information transfer and processing is heavily dependent upon language. Mathematics has much specialist vocabulary, including that applied to abstract and complex concepts, as well as using some 'everyday' vocabulary with more specific and restricted meanings. Durkin and Shire (1991) and Pimm (1991) suggested that words first encountered in a non-mathematical context (e.g. above, difference, figure, make, right, table, value) could cause particular difficulties for children owing to their ambiguity. The potential for confusion is enormous.

The linguistic aspect of learning mathematical concepts is thus of particular importance (Choat 1981). Concept formation is aided greatly by the ability to use the related language, while the learning of new concepts is closely associated with the acquisition of new words which are meaningful. Children might learn words without really understanding the associated concepts, while their understanding of some concepts might be underestimated because they do not use the 'official' terminology. Jones & Haylock (1985) described activities in which children used language in the course of mathematical activities in ways that were meaningful to them. They emphasised the value of this with the slogan 'understanding means making connections' – between the concrete–motor, linguistic, pictorial and symbolic aspects of mathematics. Correspondingly, too heavy a reliance on the medium of language in the process of teaching mathematics is likely to differentially disadvantage children whose language is not well developed.

In Paired Maths projects the need for the children to use and understand words and phrases in a mathematical context, through the discussion of joint and purposeful concrete activities, is strongly emphasised to both parents and peers (and through them, to teachers). One of the advantages of mathematical games is that they readily stimulate related discussion.

Maths games

At least at a superficial level, parents and teachers are likely to have some shared understanding of what 'reading' is. This is much less likely with mathematics, however, as maths is a much larger and more varied area – certainly not a unitary skill. Asking parents to 'do maths' with their children therefore holds greater possibilities for confusion and harm, and stronger support or scaffolding of the parent–child interaction is needed. The structured rules and materials of games provide this, while the choice of games avoids any danger of an autocratic 'top–down' ethos likely to disempower the participants.

As much research has shown (e.g. Hughes 1983, Rogers and Miller 1984), if mathematical content can be contained in play form, motivation for learning will be so powerful that the question of 'relevance' will never arise for the child. Skemp (1989a,b) specifically devised games to provide shared experiences which gave rise to mathematical discussion among the children. The peer group interaction was seen as an important method of learning and much less threatening than being told what was wrong by the teacher. Skemp found his materials provided a focus for in-service training for teachers, which improved their own mathematical knowledge as well as providing insight into how children learn.

Many advantages have been claimed for a gaming approach to mathematics (e.g. Kirkby 1992). It is argued that games promote active involvement, are intrinsically motivating, exciting and challenging, and help avoid boredom. They are grounded in concrete meaningful experience and have a purpose in which the child is intimately engaged, promoting decision-making and problem-solving. Concentration and persistence can be far greater than for 'traditional' mathematical activities, increasing time on task. They enable a grasp of mathematical concepts to be deployed, demonstrated and practised before children are ready to grapple with symbols and recording. They can require children to think and do more calculations mentally than they could possibly record on paper in the same time. They facilitate repetition for consolidation without tedium. Success or failure is self-evident, so they are self-correcting – no 'marking' is required. The extent to which games can be played at different levels and the element of chance enable children of all abilities to be included and all children to have an equal likelihood of success. The inherent enjoyment and success can foster positive attitudes to the self and to mathematics – hopefully generalising to other situations and other types of activity. They can stimulate creativity and imagination and encourage team cooperation in learning. And, of course, they stimulate related discussion, and help develop communication, turn-taking and other interpersonal skills.

Games were adopted in Paired Maths to provide meaningful shared activities yielding practical experience of underlying mathematical concepts without the need for elaborate training. The emphasis was on activities which were intrinsically enjoyable, in order to create the opportunity for attitude change in children and parents alike. They enabled the matching of prediction against outcome, experience against expectation, in activities in which the children could learn from and compare ideas with their parents, but in the context of an equality between partners forced by games of chance. Overlying all of this was the importance of the opportunity to explore the pragmatic use of the language of mathematics through the activities.

There are, however, no universal panaceas, and the nature and quality of the games is all-important. Many 'maths games' accompanying commercially-published school-based maths schemes are utterly dreary and pedagogically inept. Those embarking on a Paired Maths project must choose the games with great discrimination and care.

Cooperative learning in maths and science

There has been a sustained interest in cooperative learning in North America, which has resulted in numerous structured cooperative learning projects, some of them involving mathematics. In Britain, cooperative learning at school level is generally less structured, sometimes applied loosely to almost any form of 'working together', with the attendant danger that children might work in groups but not as a group.

For proponents of specific, structured, well-researched methods for cooperative learning (e.g. Slavin 1990), cooperative learning is about 'structuring positive interdependence'. It is 'more than working together. It implies synergy, a combined action of differentiated specialists' (Topping 1992). Cooperative learning should at least involve small groups in which students have to jointly organise their time and resources to work towards some specific shared goal. For instance, the whole task might be divided into specialist areas in which one group member becomes expert, and then everyone's 'new' knowledge and skills are 'jigsawed' back together to achieve the joint goal. Slavin (1990) proposed that in addition to group goals and task specialisation, cooperative learning should occur in groups of heterogeneous ability and also be characterised by individual accountability, equal opportunities for success, team competition and adaptation to individual needs. Paired Maths and cross-ability Paired Science in the peer group setting meet these requirements.

The foremost name in small group cooperative learning in mathematics is that of Neil Davidson, who has provided several reviews of research (Davidson 1985, 1989; Davidson and Kroll 1991) and a handbook of readings for teachers (Davidson 1990). Various other authors have provided cooperative learning lesson plans for mathematics. For example, Jasmine and Jasmine (1996) describe a range of activities under the headings of:

- attributes and classification,
- understanding numbers and numeration,
- understanding arithmetic operations,
- visualising and representing shapes,
- dealing with data,

- location and mapping,
- the process of measurement,
- geometric figures, and
- games and rules – complete with worksheets.

Dees and her colleagues (1989) offered something similar but more varied.

However, the vast majority of reports on cooperative learning in mathematics indicate a high degree of structuring directly by the class teacher, often based on relatively traditional materials. Mathematical games are rarely mentioned, except as a 'filler' activity.

Peer tutoring in maths and science

Peer tutoring differs from cooperative learning in that it is characterised by specific role-taking: at any point someone has the job of tutor or helper while the other (or the others) are in role as tutee(s). Quite specific procedures for interaction might also be outlined, in which the participants are likely to have training which is specific or generic or both. Both members of the pair should find some cognitive challenge in their joint activities and the tutor should be 'learning by teaching'. Gains for both helpers and helped are targeted: double added value.

Although there are a number of reports of peer tutoring in maths in the international literature, many in the USA have involved highly structured drill and practice routines in which the tutor merely apes the role of a traditional teacher, while those involving mathematical games have tended to be descriptive and omit substantive evaluation (see Chapter 6 for a more detailed discussion).

In Scotland, cross-age peer tutoring in mathematics of 8–9-year-olds by 12-year-olds in a primary school using methods and materials drawn from the regular school mathematics curriculum was reported by Renwick (1995, personal communication). Mathematically-able tutors were paired with able tutees, and less able tutors with less able tutees. The tutors visited the tutees' class weekly and worked with gender-balanced groups of three tutees, but each group of tutees was assigned three tutors, thus engaging in three half-hour sessions per week. Video process data was gathered but no outcome evaluation reported.

Parental involvement in maths internationally

Turning now to parental involvement, various types of programmes to involve parents and other carers in the mathematical development of their children have become more common throughout the world, but perhaps particularly since the start of the 1990s in North America.

Reports offering a wealth of organisational detail are highlighted here. A series of six workshops for parents were described by Goldberg (1990), reviewing mathematical activities usable in the home with the aim of improving achievement in and attitudes toward maths for 8–12-year-old children. A substantial guide for parents in Australia was developed by Costello *et al.* (1991), emphasising mathematics in everyday life and the importance of discussion and language. Home activities for children aged 5 to 13 and their parents were detailed by Kanter *et al.* (1992) in a booklet published by the US Department of Education, with an emphasis on communication and developing positive attitudes.

Owens (1992) produced the delightfully titled *Parent-Helper Book for Those Who Want Arithmetic Made Touchable*, which in fact also covered geometry and other areas and included detailed activity guidelines. 'Natural Math' was a programme offered to preschool and kindergarten Seminole and Chickasaw Head Start Native American and African American families (Sears and Medearis 1992, 1993, and see Chapter 4), utilising activities and games developed to relate to the home culture. The 'Family Math' programme (see Appendices 3 and 5) has proved very popular in the USA and Canada and has extended to parts of Australia (Onslow 1992, and see Chapter 4).

Martin (1993) focused on parents in adult literacy classes, creating take-home parent and child activity kits designed for use with everyday materials, launched via parent workshops and including instruction sheets in Spanish. Planning and organisation considerations in establishing parent–teacher partnerships in mathematics were outlined by Neil (1994). 'Beyond Facts and Flashcards' was the evocative title of a parent guide produced by Mokros (1996), designed to help parents uncover the mathematics in their daily lives through everyday experiences, suggesting many activities. Similar creations had come earlier from Valentine (1992), Leonard and Tracy (1993) and Sharp *et al.* (1995).

However, with the exception of the long-standing Family Math programme, similar developments had begun somewhat earlier in the UK.

Parental involvement in maths in the UK

Following the surge in interest in parental involvement in reading at the beginning of the 1980s, a ripple effect became discernible in mathematics. By 1983 Jennings had published 'Mathematics in the secondary school: a programme of support involving parents', which was a report on parental involvement in maths with high school pupils, and a number of postgraduate research theses followed (e.g. Paskin 1986, Risk 1988).

Set in a deprived multicultural urban area of West Yorkshire, Alan Graham's 'Sums for Mums' project, coupled with his book 'Help Your Child With Maths' (Graham 1985), was another major development. The project targeted women and aimed to enhance their self-esteem as mathematicians with onward transmission to their daughters, this focus reflecting funding by the Equal Opportunities Commission. Although set in local schools, the workshop sessions were oriented to adult learners, and eschewed 'conventional textbook maths'. This was followed by Parent Resource in Support of Maths (PRISM). However, little substantive summative evaluation was reported. Nevertheless, Graham's (1985) book remains a major resource in the area.

The IMPACT project, widely known in the UK, involves the class teacher sending home mathematical activities which parent and child carry out together (Merttens and Vass 1987, 1993). It is closely tied to traditional classroom activities which the child exports to the home, often involving whole classes completing the same 'homework' simultaneously. This enables the activity to be closely articulated to current class teaching, but is a more 'top–down' approach. Surprisingly, given its high profile, little evaluation evidence on IMPACT other than the anecdotal appears to be publicly available (Merttens and Vass 1993).

Projects more akin to Paired Maths have sprung up in various parts of the country. One such is the 'Play Along Maths' programme described by Cheyne (1994, personal communication), a Home School Community Tutor. The programme targets families when children are just beginning school. Activities and games (including jigsaws and peg games, all cross-referenced to the prescribed 5–14 Curriculum) are sent home, coupled with 'activity cards' bearing ideas and rules prepared by volunteer parents. Much emphasis is placed on language, under the rubric of 'Chat-Along', and essential vocabulary amounting to 200 words is mapped out. Each game or activity is used for 10 to 15 minutes per day for a week, then changed. Families keep diaries noting the game/activity, day, time and any comments – children adding smiley faces if they liked the game.

The objectives, history and development of Paired Maths

The developers of Paired Maths were aware of the long-standing evidence that parental attitudes, expectations and behaviour had a significant effect on their children's educational progress. A surge in enthusiasm for parental involvement in reading at the beginning of the 1980s led to the description in the international literature of a variety of methods for parental involvement and peer tutoring in literacy (Topping and Wolfendale 1985, Wolfendale and Topping 1996).

The Kirklees Psychological Service in the Kirklees Education Authority in West Yorkshire had already recognised the effectiveness of involving parents in children's education by funding projects on a permanent basis. For example, the Portage Project, aimed at helping parents of preschool children with disabilities to teach them in their own homes, was well established.

Projects to encourage parents to help their children's reading at home became an increasingly widespread feature of home and school cooperation. In Kirklees, specific structured methods such as Paired Reading, Cued Spelling and Paired Writing were designed or extended and evaluated (see Topping 1995). These methods proved very effective, durable and easy for schools to use, and spread to a majority of schools in the authority.

Attention turned to the possibility of parental involvement in other curricular areas, and the Multiply Attainments Through Home Support (MATHS) project was launched in Kirklees – the beginnings of Paired Maths as reported in this book. Many schools had already been successful with Paired Reading, and from this foundation were confident to proceed with Paired Maths.

The main aim of the first Paired Maths project was to find out whether a home-based maths project could have similar positive effects to those already obtained with home reading projects. The project leaders sought to identify the crucial organisational elements of the successful home reading projects, and to incorporate these into the design for a home maths project. The elements hypothesised as important were:

- regular home-school liaison,
- regular (but short) parent–child sessions at home,
- loosely structured tasks,
- regular recording by parents,
- a contract for involvement over a limited period, and
- a relaxed attitude towards the task(s) by parent–child–teacher.

As with other paired methods, the delivery of a first Paired Maths project in collaboration with a school was also intended as a form of participatory in-service training for the teachers. The activities and format were designed to be non-threatening to either teachers or parents, both in content and teaching implications. The projects aimed to reinforce for teachers, through explication to parents, the importance of language and non-computational activities in understanding and practising mathematical concepts. This form of in-service training was thus both direct and indirect, applied to the teachers through the parents. The Psychological Service aimed to ensure that the parents and teachers were successful and then faded out, leaving the key players at the grass roots convinced that success was attributable largely to their own efforts and confident to continue with minimal further support.

Unlike the paired approaches in literacy, Paired Maths used specified materials (games), necessitated by the width and complexity of the area and the very limited confidence of many parents (and teachers) in it. Kits of mathematical games were assembled for this purpose, which were loaned to schools as part of 'pump-priming', after which schools were expected to create their own in-house kit for subsequent projects.

Much of the early Paired Maths work involved parental tutoring, using kits of mathematical games appropriate to children aged 4 to 7 (Year 0–2 children in National Curriculum Key Stage 1; P1 to P3 in Scotland). Projects were generally targeted on mixed-ability classes in mainstream schools, rather than on children with difficulties, this being necessitated by principles of equal opportunity and serving to avoid any stigmatisation.

Later, the contents of this Key Stage 1 kit was revised, and kits different in structure and content were developed for 'junior' age children (7 to 11 years, Key Stage 2), and for lower secondary age children (11 to 13 years, Key Stage 3), with the expectation that older children would be increasingly likely to use these in peer-based projects in schools. Peer and parent projects began to be operated across this wider age range.

Many more schools showed interest in developing projects, including schools for children with learning difficulties. In multicultural schools, the language content of Paired Maths was found very valuable for families whose first language was not English. A Handbook was produced for extra-district enquirers, and very favourable publicity in the national press resulted in the distribution of well over 1,600 of these manuals worldwide.

In parallel, the extension of 'paired learning' into science was undertaken, particularly for parent tutoring of children aged 4 to 7, 'scaffolded' by a combination of detailed activity sheets and practical materials which could be found in the home or loaned by the school (see *The Paired Science Handbook*, Topping 1998).

Why Paired Maths is different

There are strong indications that maths games, cooperative learning in maths, peer tutoring in maths and parental involvement in maths can all be effective separately (see Chapter 4).

The Paired Maths method seeks to blend selected elements of all these approaches together to create an especially powerful package – novel in its combination more than in its elements.

In any case, one swallow does not make a summer – some positive reports in the literature do not necessarily indicate a methodology which can be implemented easily and successfully in everyday life in many varied schools.

The Paired Maths method seeks to blend these selected elements into a package which is robust and durable as well as effective – lending itself to widespread replication in many different contexts with minimal resource requirements.

We have seen that Paired Maths has a strong emphasis on discussion and language and on concrete hands-on activity, with a de-emphasis on written recording. As will become clearer in Chapter 2, it includes games which can be played in different ways and at different levels of abstraction and complexity, offering choice from a pool of activities structured to ensure experience of a breadth of mathematical experiences, avoiding a narrow preoccupation with number. It blends cooperation and competition, operating through cognitive conflict between equal (or equalised) partners and also through apprenticeship with a more capable partner.

The particularly distinctive features of the organisational system of Paired Maths include:

- a very strong focus on developing more positive attitudes to mathematics and to the self as a mathematician (increasing enthusiasm and confidence) in all participants (child or adult), rather than a preoccupation with specific official maths knowledge. Extending the mathematical 'comfort zone' and lowering anxiety increases disclosure, identification and correction of misconception. Maths is about feelings, too.
- a very strong focus on the value of the existing home and community mathematical culture and competencies, with the aim of building on those competencies to enable parents and children to meet their own needs, not just the needs of the school system. It seeks to leave participants with a greater sense of ownership and control over their own environment. Maths is for life.
- an emphasis on self-selection and choice for maximum individualisation and

personal relevance, and through that the highest possible levels of motivation. Maths is about me.

- a systemic approach involving reciprocal interaction and feedback with inbuilt intrinsic rewards for all players – thus creating a self-sustaining virtuous circle (for the teachers, too). Everybody helps everybody, consciously or otherwise. No-one is as smart as all of us.
- a systemic approach which enables the offering of equal opportunities and access to all members of all families of all kinds. We all get to play.

Thus the Paired Maths system blends selected elements of good practice together into a package which is robust and dynamic as well as inclusive and effective, with a particular focus on feelings, relevance to individual life needs and mutual and lifelong learning. All of this is also true of Paired Science.

Implications for Paired Science

Indeed, much of the discussion in this chapter relates to Paired Science just as much as to Paired Maths. Given these many commonalities, this final section merely elaborates points of difference.

As Paired Maths grew, parental involvement in science was soon seen as the next fertile ground for development, with many inherent advantages. Early years children involved in science investigations at home would certainly be relating scientific ideas and skills to their own real-life situation in the company of mature and highly-valued adults. They could have their own personal demonstrations of what to do if all else failed. They would have the opportunity to explore their nascent understanding through discussion, enjoying immediate feedback and possibly improving their general language development as well as their scientific vocabulary. Apart from the extra practice, generalisation and transferability would be developed, but even more importantly, this activity could serve to improve the child's motivation, confidence and self-image.

Clearly, capability in science is as useful and important as capability in maths, not only for the aspirations of the individual, but also for the economic well-being of the nation. 'Capability' implies the ability to generalise analytical thinking and transferable skills in science out of the classroom and into everyday life to solve real problems. Paired Science seeks to do this.

Currently there is less concern about standards of attainment in science in the UK than there is about standards in mathematics. The TIMMS survey accorded England fourth place out of 25 countries in science tests – much better than their performance in mathematics (e.g. Scottish Office 1996a). The performance of the 10 per cent most able was comparatively even better. Scotland did better than England in Maths, but less well in science. However, science and maths inevitably go together – at higher levels, competence in one without competence in the other becomes unsustainable.

As in maths, gender differentials in science performance seem less than traditionally has been expected. In England and Scotland, boys tended to score higher than girls, but the difference reached statistical significance only in one of the four areas of science tested in England. However, science remains proportionally over-chosen by boys at post-16 education, so girls might still not be fulfilling their potential in this respect.

Paired Science is always organised on a nominally cross-ability basis – someone is supposed to be the helper, the other the learner. Thus we might assume that Paired Science is more likely to operate according to Vygotskian principles than Piagetian ones. However, this would be an over-simplification, since children can certainly generate cognitive conflict and challenge for their parents in this area, not least by asking penetrating questions which demand a simple explanation of an abstract and complex concept. Parents and other tutors should not expect to be omniscient and will certainly 'learn by teaching'.

The role of language in Paired Science is crucial, just as in the early stages of learning mathematics. To support the helper in this, each Activity Sheet has lots of questions, and the helpers are asked to raise these, then help the child to work out the answer for themselves. In addition, throughout the text of the Activity Sheet, some key words of scientific vocabulary are printed in bold. These are important words in science and the helpers are asked to use them and talk about them as much as possible during the activity.

Compared to 'maths games' (which can have the disadvantage of not being initially seen as 'proper maths'), the Paired Science activities have a higher face validity for parents and other users – they look more like 'proper science' and might therefore be more immediately acceptable. However, there are attendant dangers – the Activity Sheets might for the same reason more readily be seen as an extension of the school and a form of 'homework', predisposing the family or other pair to a weary and tokenistic response.

However, the scaffolding provided by the Activity Sheets is certainly necessary, even when operating Paired Science within the classroom. Although there is an increasing volume of information and research about cooperative learning in science in the classroom (e.g. Graves and Graves 1991), early years children have limited independent research skills and group investigations can easily end up with 'the blind leading the blind'. Even were this not the case, generalisation of transferable scientific skills outside the classroom to real-life problems would remain a major difficulty.

Parental involvement in science has become a growth area in the UK in recent years. Commercial companies are waiting to capitalise on any parental anxiety, and a number of books and materials for parents on helping children with science at home are now available (e.g. Young and Young 1991). Given this interest, a number of initiatives developed. The School Home Investigations in Primary Science (SHIPS) project was modelled upon the long-standing IMPACT maths approach. The SHIPS team noted that much existing science material had an unthinking 'recipe' approach to yield the 'right' answer, and were concerned to devise activities which could be approached in a number of different ways (Solomon and Lee 1991). Following IMPACT methodology, the expectation was that each half term the class teacher would prepare all the children for the same activity, which they (hopefully) carried out in the same week at home with their parents. This clearly maximises curriculum linkage and the opportunities for subsequent whole-class discussion and review of everyone's experiences. However, it could seem rather too much like old-fashioned 'homework', and is perhaps at risk of being accused of pedagogical imperialism and a failure to fully value the culture and capabilities of the home.

A team of community educators in Humberside County Council have been extremely prolific and innovative in producing resources for parental involvement over the years. Their *Parental Involvement in Science* pack (Chambers *et al.* 1992) deliberately sets out to emphasise the 'fun' element in science, including tasks such as 'design and build a shelter into which four members of the family can fit, using only newspaper and sellotape' and 'devise a test to see what kind of carrier bag is the best'. The number of activities outlined is not large, as the intention is to lead teachers into creating their own ideas. The linkage to the curriculum is perhaps less obvious than in the SHIPS approach, but the motivational power seems likely to be high. The materials are illustrated with cartoons and there is discussion of the social management of introductory meetings with parents.

Similar developments were occurring elsewhere in the world. The Great Explorations in Math and Science (GEMS) programme in the USA produced a Parent's Guide to GEMS in 1991. The US Government offered a publication titled *Math, Science, and Your Daughter: What Can Parents Do?* (Campbell 1992). The American Chemical Society's Education Division created the Parents and Children for Terrific Science PACTS programme. Rillero (1994) reviewed the emerging field. In Australia, Science PACT (based on the maths IMPACT programme in the UK) developed (search the Internet for current website).

In this developing field, the distinctive features of Paired Science are worth reiterating, albeit briefly since they are very similar to those for Paired Maths:

- strong focus on developing positive attitudes (feelings),
- strong focus on existing home and community scientific culture and competencies (life needs),
- emphasis on self-selection and choice (personal relevance),
- reciprocal interaction and feedback with rewards for all (gains for all),
- equal opportunities and access for all.

The Paired Science system is engineered to be robust and dynamic as well as inclusive and effective – it is structured but flexible.

CHAPTER 2

Materials: selecting and creating maths games

This chapter explores the elements necessary for games to be successful in providing opportunities to work with a variety of mathematical concepts. The different categories used within the National Curriculum levels are described and the rationale for the choice of games and the mathematical subskills they aim to develop are outlined. A variety of ways of acquiring and/or producing a kit of games are discussed. Materials for Paired Science are then discussed.

Principles behind successful games

In his model of mathematics as an activity of our intelligence, Skemp (1989a) suggests that mathematical concepts are learned through schema building and schema testing – building up expectations of the way things behave and then testing out those ideas when new opportunities occur. Thus, we get ideas from each other which we try out against our own. We need to experience and experiment, to communicate and to discuss, and be able to use imagination and creativity to generalise and abstract, in order to determine what will remain constant.

The revised programmes of study and attainment targets for the English and Welsh National Curriculum in mathematics became legal requirements by means of an order made by the Secretaries of State for Education and for Wales, coming into effect on 1 August 1995 for all year groups in Key Stages 1, 2 and 3. The first section, 'Using and applying mathematics', identifies ways of developing the skills necessary to tackle unfamiliar problems and processes used in mathematics (Department for Education and Employment 1995).

In this, three strands are proposed:

- mathematical decision-making – linking one idea with another,
- communicating – encouraging children to talk about their thinking,
- reasoning mathematically, which focuses on generalising mathematical relationships – the most difficult skill to develop.

The use of games and puzzles can provide the opportunities for all these relationships and skills to be developed and consolidated.

The first Paired Maths projects followed the Paired Reading format of involving parents and children for ten minutes daily. However the most obvious difference was the basis of the Paired Maths involvement. For reading there had always been a large pool of material waiting to be read. The local library was likely to be happy to help, and the school (with the support of the School Library Service) would be able to provide access to a range of suitable books for home loan. With Paired Maths, however, there was no immediate source of materials ready and available for parents to borrow. The solution was maths games.

In the context of parent–child interaction, games can provide more opportunities to explore ideas and more opportunities for communication and discussion than is normally available in the classroom. As Durkin (1993) expressed it: 'the only reason a preschool child is likely to want to know how many things there are of something is that someone else asked'. It is important that the activities are enjoyable, both in order that the parents and children can relax while engaged in a mathematical activity, and so that the motivation to continue will be high. Games also help to stimulate the use of mathematical language, especially if this is pre-structured as it is in Paired Maths (see Chapter 3).

Games and puzzles have a number of other advantages. They:

- can be seen as part of normal home experiences,
- are highly motivating because the child is actively participating and is in control,
- involve immediate feedback and an element of competition,
- have well-defined limits and directions,
- are meaningful experiences, somewhere between concrete reality and the abstract world,
- can be used to consolidate class work or to encourage and enable a child to extend his or her skills,
- can be fun for parents too!

Experience showed that ideally games should meet the following criteria. They should:

- be enjoyable,
- allow equal competition or cooperation between child and parent,
- be easy to understand,
- be flexible and allow extension,
- encourage discussion,
- be robust – both physically and in minimising a didactic approach,
- not look like school work,
- be attractive,
- be well packaged and easily kept together,
- be inexpensive.

The balance between competition or cooperation is an important one. Some mathematical games are solely skills based and therefore put the child (presumed to be the one with lesser skills) at a disadvantage when playing with a parent. They might also tempt the more 'able' partner to take on an overt teaching role, which is not one of the aims of the project. Therefore, the majority of games chosen can be won through luck only, but do require certain mathematical skills while playing. Other games pose mathematical problems which are novel to both child and partner and hence allow equal cooperation.

Beasley (1990) outlined four classes of games in mathematics:

- games of pure chance,
- games of mixed chance and skill,
- games of pure skill,
- automatic games.

In Paired Maths there are games of chance that include most of the dice and spinner games, games such as Yahtzee which mix chance and skill, games of skill which include many of the strategy games and puzzles, and games combining chance and strategy with an automatic element (such as Uno).

The games need to be attractively produced so that the children want to use them. If they involve as many as possible of the senses (through activities such as speaking, listening, watching, touching, moving and even smelling and tasting), they are likely to be accessible to more children of different abilities and cultural and linguistic backgrounds. However, they should not incorporate irrelevant distraction. They need to be durable: solidly constructed and packaged so that they are not easily broken by young, enthusiastic users. They should not have too many loose or small parts which are easy to scatter and lose, which might be difficult to manipulate, or which might be unsafe in the hands of younger members of the family.

They should not be too big, or they will prove difficult to store and transport home. The game itself should be reasonably brief – not every child can wait hours for a conclusion. Games need clear rules for play which are not too long, nor too difficult to read or follow – and the game does need to have a clear sense of purpose. Obviously, the games chosen should be appropriate to the chronological age or developmental level of the children who will be playing them. However, it is even better if they can be played at various different levels of complexity.

Choosing the games in the beginning

Enjoyment is the basic premise in the choice of games for Paired Maths. The actual activities have to encompass those elements of mathematics which can be developed further at home and yet which are robust enough to be used in many different ways. In addition the activities have to be capable of being used at various levels of development and, most importantly, have to be enjoyable.

The first project was aimed at Key Stage 1 children aged 5 to 7, and used adaptations of games, each incorporating different aspects of 'number'. The English National Curriculum Level 1 description of 'number' competencies is probably fairly typical: 'Pupils count, order, add and subtract numbers when solving problems involving up to ten objects. They read and write the numbers involved. Pupils recognise and make repeating patterns, counting the number of objects in each repeat'.

The first four basic games chosen were Rows, Rods, Cards and Tangrams.

Tangrams is an old Chinese puzzle which involves regular shapes which can be aligned to form a square (shape, position and comparison). It is available in plastic pieces which are good to handle and need just an element of competition to make into a game for two. Either a spinner for choice of pieces or 'turns' to see who is the last person to complete is required.

Rods involved a selection of coloured rods each with a regular relationship to the others, providing concrete number experience (pattern, size and relationships). These were made up from old sets of wooden Cuisenaire rods of various lengths, showing the properties of various numbers (now available in plastic). They provide experience of numbers in a wonderful solid form that could make many games: taking turns, making steps or walls, copying patterns or picture outlines, perhaps using a dice or spinner to add an element of competition.

Cards involved a pack of normal playing cards with ideas for activities extending their use, including Snap, Rummy, and Pelmanism (Counting, Sorting and Groups). Parents proved to be very good at extending and devising new ideas.

Rows involved coloured counters which could be put into a frame to make both vertical and horizontal patterns. The game could be extended with the use of a dice, and further extended (e.g. Four in a Row) to explore wider aspects of reflection and symmetry (matching, orientation and discrimination).

Each game was accompanied by a list of activities to do with the materials, a list of words to be used and a Record Sheet. Parents were encouraged to use all the words each session and asked to note down which were actually used.

Development of the games kits

The early evaluations highlighted the need to extend the number and variety of games. Accordingly, a larger bank of suitable games was collected. Initially this was based on suggestions from parents involved in the pilot project, colleagues in the Maths Advisory Team, Professor Skemp who was instrumental in encouraging and supporting the development, and from catalogues and publishers who were prepared to donate possible games. Eventually over 40 different games were accumulated.

So far the mathematical element of the games has hardly been mentioned, because once the decision is made to look for the mathematics that is already there, the most interesting and enjoyable games on the toyshop shelves are the ones which are likely to have the mathematical elements to provide the experience and exploration that Paired Maths aims to encourage. Even the traditional games that grandparents remember playing before the days of television (e.g. Ludo, Snakes and Ladders, Dominoes, Beetle and Draughts) all provide opportunities for meaningful counting, one-to-one matching and addition.

Key Stage 1

The English National Curriculum has divided mathematics into three major fields for children in the 5 to 7 age group (Key Stage 1):

1. Using and applying mathematics,
2. Number,
3. Shape, Space and Measures,
4. Handling data (this fourth topic is introduced formally after children reach the age of 7, linking into Key Stage 2).

The emphasis is on flexibility and the use of a variety of resources and methods. Much of the work in mathematics is related to the real world and other curriculum topics that the children may be studying. Each aspect of the mathematics curriculum has elements that can be readily addressed through appropriate discussion of the language that directly arises from playing games, for example:

Using and applying Maths

Understanding the language of Mathematics – words and phrases such as triangle, bigger than, next to . . . .

Number

- Know the names of the numbers and be able to count, 1–2–3–4.
- Sort and classify a set of objects according to their size or shape (grouping bigger and smaller things into piles).

Shape, Space and Measure

- Understanding and using the properties of shape.
- Understanding and using properties of position and movement.

In order to accommodate this emphasis on language the games can be grouped under the headings of early mathematical concepts which the children will meet in class:

Key Stage 1 Games Categories

Matching	Shape	Pattern
Ordering	Counting	Conservation

The six basic categories at the Key Stage 1 level relate neatly to a six-week project in which participants are asked to choose one game from a different category each week. For ease of differentiation, each category was colour-coded, so participants knew a red-coded game had to be returned to the red-coded box, and that they could not then take another red game. This ensured that they sampled a wide range of mathematical activities and avoided reinforcing a narrow conceptualisation of what maths entails and embraces. It also enabled the mathematical language in play with each game to be focused on a limited set of highly relevant key words. This was more manageable for the parents, and over the whole project children would be cumulatively exposed to the complete range of language. An outline of the core mathematical vocabulary covered across all categories will be found in *The Paired Maths Handbook* (Topping and Bamford 1998) in Section B6.

Although games were chosen because they were fun and for their face validity (i.e. they had obvious mathematical elements) they were categorised by their most prominent conceptual content. However, many games actually cover more than one conceptual area of mathematics, and could be categorised in more than one. Nevertheless, in order to offer the children as wide a range of language as possible the games are placed (somewhat arbitrarily) into one of the six mathematical categories.

Well-known games with an element of luck and competition such as Snakes and Ladders, Ludo and card games are all easily accommodated under counting and matching. Other more recent commercial games were also included, alongside those which had been locally devised. An example of the latter was Pass the Bag – a game that involves feeling for wooden geometrical shapes inside a bag. The shapes then have to be matched to a card where the template might be a different size or colour. Such a game obviously comes under the category of Shape, but would also include matching, relationships and, to some extent, strategy. Pattern and relationships underpinned all the concepts that were included, since they form the basis of problem-solving and as such permeate every aspect of mathematics.

Key Stage 1 – Suggestions for games

Counting	Matching	Shape
Snakes and Ladders	Three to Match	Pass the Bag
Ludo	Huff Puff	Shapes
Insey Winsey Spider	Humpty Dumpty	Tessellation
Scaredy Cat	Memo	Mr Space Game
Beggar my Neighbour	Dominoes	Tangrams
Blackpool card game	Beetle	Jigsaw
Leapfrog	Snap (various forms)	Attribute Bingo
Cat and Mouse	Bingo	Dotty Triangles

Pattern	Conservation	Ordering
Ladybirds	Rods	Rummy
Pick a Button	Button Box	Halves and Quarters
Mosaics	Connect 4 (Rows)	The Old Woman who Lived
Happy Families	Dogimoes	in a Shoe
3 Men's Morris	Choose a Pattern	Hundred Square Jigsaw
Nine Holes	Three at a Time	Crossing Game
		Beanstalk/Dragon

Where there was a smaller number of games in a category, two of each kind were included. The number of games rather than the range within the boxes is the important element and will depend on the number of children involved. A fuller description of some of these Key Stage 1 games will be found in Appendix 1a of this book. In *The Paired Maths Handbook* (Topping and Bamford 1998), Section B11 is a reproducible handout which outlines the National Curriculum linkages in further detail for this level.

Key Stage 2

The categories for the next level, Key Stage 2 (children aged 7 to 11), were somewhat different.

Key Stage 2 – Games categories

Bonds	Shape	Strategy
Relationships	Puzzles (cross-area)	

The alterations in categorisation from Key Stage 1 reflect developmental patterns of mathematical growth in children, and the related difference in Key Stage 2 terminology in the National Curriculum. The early emphasis on Conservation, Matching and Counting was seen as leading to work on Number Bonds and Relationships. The early emphasis on Ordering and Pattern led toward Strategy. The Shape category remained, at a higher level of operation. Puzzles were included as examples of cross-area activities. A choice is left from any area for the sixth week.

A full listing of the titles of games included in the Paired Maths Key Stage 2 kits will be found in Appendix 1b in this book.

Key Stage 3

For Key Stage 3, the games kits were extended so that rather than being taken home they could form the basis of peer group interaction in class. The categorical structure showed further change from the kits for younger children.

Key Stage 3 – Games categories

Number games	Space games	Strategy games
Solitaire or Cooperative puzzles		Extension games

Each of the boxes of games included an extended number of games in order to allow for a frequent exchange in a full class session. Given constraints of expense and storage in creating kits including large numbers of three-dimensional games, a modest number of these games were supplemented by a substantial quantity of two-dimensional games. Many of these latter can be readily produced using card and plastic laminate. Some were based on ancient games from many world cultures, some on games of more recent origin in the public domain, and some were created for the purpose. A full listing of these will be found in Appendix 1c in this book, and some examples to reproduce and use directly will be found in *The Paired Maths Handbook* (Topping and Bamford 1998) in Section C.

The games were mainly oriented toward the lower end of Key Stage 3, but an extension category was provided. The Number category included Counting, Number Bonds, Sequence, Ordering, Computation (arithmetic) and Probability. There was little emphasis on Measurement – games cannot (and perhaps should not try to) do everything. Strategy games involved a large element of deduction and prediction leading to the generation of strategies, in many cases requiring an algebraic understanding of the mathematical principles involved. Space games incorporated a large element of visuo-spatial perception and organisation, an appreciation of shape, pattern and geometry, in two and three dimensions and with reference to solids, and including locations and transformation in space.

Puzzles covered all areas explored in the interactive game format by the categories above. Some were very hard! The increased emphasis on individual puzzles ensured that where there is a heterogeneous group, and perhaps erratic attendance patterns, individuals can operate alone at certain times. However, many of these 'solitaire' puzzles prove fascinating to others, and cooperative problem-solving pairs or groups can often form spontaneously even without teacher suggestion. In these games the discussion becomes directed along the lines of why and how the puzzle works and how it could be improved.

The 'extension' group was a cross-area collection of more challenging interactive games for more mathematically able or persistent pupils, preferably working in pairs of similar ability. They mainly covered Space and Strategy at a higher level. For one group of pupils the promise of answers upon application led to mass letter writing to the manufacturers, asking for the answers which had eluded even their teachers.

All five boxes required skills in data handling and the organisation of information (although not necessarily written record-keeping) and skill in the application and generalisation of mathematical principles. Categories other than Strategy included activities with some strategic elements. Calculator use was suggested for some games in some categories. In relation to National Curriculum requirements, the Key Stage 3 kit was particularly strong on application and approximation, prediction and probability, strategy and spatial aspects – and especially on problem-solving at speed. The kit was relatively light on written recording, decimals, fractions, percentages, measuring and working with very large numbers. In *The Paired Maths Handbook* (Topping and Bamford 1998), Section B12 is a reproducible handout which outlines the National Curriculum linkages in greater detail for this level.

Sources of games

The development of kits of games came about because although schools were very keen to involve parents in the extension of their children's mathematics, they could not immediately produce sufficient games for a whole class group to be involved. Kits were therefore made available centrally which could be borrowed by schools for an initial project, to explore whether the parents and children would be keen to be involved. These provided a means of identifying popular games in each school's catchment area and clarifying what would be needed. Once the initial project was underway, schools involved parents in fund-raising, making games, searching car boot sales and writing to manufacturers for sample games in order to provide their own kits for future projects.

Many games are commercially available. Some of these are for four people and can be split into two, providing two sets to borrow. However, manufacturers are constantly looking for novelty. Often the games are taken off the market or replaced with alternatives, so the basic principles of selection have to be applied each time a new kit is made up. More games will be found in commercial outlets in the months before Christmas – although it is difficult for teachers to find time for game hunting during this period. Many games suppliers have a mail order facility (although with the attendant problem of not being able to inspect the goods), and useful addresses will be found in Appendix 2 in this book. A list of books including mathematical games will be found in Appendix 3.

Another source of games is the North Manchester Mathematics Centre (NORMAC) and publications and ideas from their conferences (see Appendix 2). Some of the games developed by Professor Richard Skemp for use in schools are also suitable for use by parents and children at home. Increasingly, maths schemes commercially produced for schools include some 'games', and perhaps even take-home activities for 'parental involvement', but these should be scrutinised carefully, as they often prove to be two-dimensional and rather dreary and repetitive.

'The ability to solve problems is at the heart of mathematics . . . for many pupils this will require a great deal of discussion and oral work before even very simple problems can be tackled in written form' (Cockcroft 1982). Playing maths games can provide just this opportunity.

Materials for Paired Science

As with mathematics, the breadth and variety of science is so vast that it was impossible to devise some simple tutoring routine which could effectively apply to all different kinds of scientific activity irrespective of the content of the activity. Similarly, parental confidence in science was felt to be as low as that in maths and certainly lower than that in reading, so there was a need for firmer 'scaffolding' of interaction between parents/helpers and children to help ensure success for all concerned, although without forming a rigid strait-jacket or suppressing creativity. Science 'games' were not considered viable (and the prospect of experiments with random outcomes seemed somewhat alarming), so a choice of guided activities supported by take-home Activity Sheets was the preferred method.

The Paired Science materials were designed for use with children (tutees) aged 5 to 8, helped at home by parents (or in school by older peer tutors, who might be up to 11 years of age). Obviously it is very important that the 'helpers' are absolutely clear about what they have to do, or chaos may ensue. Equally obviously, busy teachers do not have the time to instruct helpers in detail. The Paired Science materials take care of this. The 45 Activity Sheets are divided into seven different areas of science closely related to National Curriculum programmes of study: Air, Magnets, Moving Things, Light, Heat, Myself and Water (see Section B3 in *The Paired Science Handbook*, Topping 1998). The Activity Sheets are the core of a well-structured procedure which is easily available to the busy teacher 'off the shelf', but which is individualised and self-managed by each active pair. Each is intended to be self-instructional for the parent or other tutor.

The simplest of equipment is required, and each Activity Sheet starts with a list of what you need. This might include items purchased by the school (such as plastic mirrors or magnets), items collected by school (such as cartons, jars or plastic bottles) and items available from school stock (card, rubber bands and glue). It might also include equipment easily found in most homes, such as a coin, a comb, a matchstick, salt, a spoon, and so on (see Section B2 in *The Paired Science Handbook*, Topping 1998).

Each Activity Sheet tells the pair what to do in simple, low readability terms. The helper is likely to read this to the child, then re-read it with discussion about meaning and implications. They can of course do Paired Reading if they wish. The practical activity can now commence, and helpers are urged to help only as much as is necessary to ensure the child eventually succeeds.

Of course, some of the helpers will themselves have limited scientific knowledge, and many will lack confidence in their scientific abilities. For whatever reason, the helper giving the child an explanation of what is happening during the activity which is completely wrong must be avoided. So the section of the Activity Sheet which is just for helpers gives them a fail-safe brief scientific explanation – with the caution that this is not to be read to the child, but to be discussed with the child if he or she fails to work it out independently through the activity.

Throughout, the role of language is crucial, just as it is in the early stages of learning mathematics. To support the helper in this, each Activity Sheet has lots of questions, and the helpers are asked to raise these, then help the child to work out the answer for themselves. In addition, throughout the text of the Activity Sheet, some key words of scientific vocabulary are printed **bold**. These are important words in science and the helpers are asked to use them and talk about them as much as possible during the activity (see Section B5 in *The Paired Science Handbook*, Topping 1998).

Each Activity Sheet includes a final section encouraging some further response from the child. This may be in terms of recording the outcome of the activity in some way, but should also encourage the child to think further about what has been learned and try to apply that understanding to different situations and problems, both in and out of school. The helpers are asked to write their own comment on the bottom of the Activity Sheet, which can then be shown to the teacher and stored in the child's Profile of Achievement. Activity Records for the whole class are easily kept by the children themselves on the chart provided (Section B4 in *The Paired Science Handbook*, Topping 1998).

Many of the design and selection principles for Paired Maths were also relevant to Paired Science. The activities had to be fun and stimulate discussion and the use of scientific language, while relating to normal home experiences and not looking like 'homework', and providing a balance of interaction and initiation between helper and helped. Activities also needed a purpose and to involve feedback – both verbally from the helper and from successful conclusion of the activity. They had to be easy to understand, flexible and allow extension, but also carry no safety risk assuming reasonable levels of responsible behaviour on the part of the helper (and child). Finally, design parameters encompassed minimal requirements for special equipment and low cost for implementation.

The present authors have frequently been asked for further Paired Science activities for older children. Time has not yet permitted this to be done, but in any event it is possible for teachers to develop their own materials using these design principles and building upon the example of the Paired Science Activity Sheets already available. Beyond this, it might be that especially creative teachers will indeed develop science 'games' to parallel the maths games. If you do either, let us know.

CHAPTER 3

Organising parental involvement in maths and science

In this chapter, the key issues involved in organising parental involvement are considered:

- establishing objectives,
- selecting target groups,
- recruiting parents,
- organising access to games or activities,
- controlling experience of various areas of mathematics or science, and
- setting up a training or 'launch' meeting.

All these aspects also apply to projects with peers, with the added issue of selection and matching of partners (see Chapter 6). Further important issues of organisation discussed in this chapter include the monitoring of the ongoing activities, trouble-shooting, feedback of evaluation results and keeping the momentum going. All these aspects are crucial and all affect the success of the outcomes for both parents and children.

The main features of parental involvement in maths and science are relatively straightforward. There needs to be a basic agreement between teacher, parent and child, and a commitment to playing maths games or doing science activities for a short period of time for several sessions per week over a period of six weeks for maths or seven weeks for science. Although the basic principles seem beguilingly simple, the organisational infrastructure necessary to support a project needs to be carefully thought through to ensure that the project will be successful. The first project must be a resounding success – for the children, the parents, the neighbourhood grapevine and (not least) for you. Start off small and invest time to ensure success for all.

Clarifying objectives

The most important aspect of any new project is the interest and determination of the head teacher. If the project is to have more than a transitory effect on one group of pupils, it is important that the reasons for embarking on the project are a clear part of the school's development plan. The objectives for the project will then be clearer, and the measures that will be needed for subsequent evaluation consequently easier to determine. By contrast, if you are unsure why you are doing it, you will not be able to determine whether it was a success or not. Objectives might be in the cognitive domain (to do with mathematical or scientific understanding, skill or achievement), the affective domain (to do with changes in attitudes or motivation), or the social domain (to do with more positive interaction and relationships). By consulting about objectives to clarify them, you help to ensure others do not have unrealistic expectations quite different from your own, which could not possibly be met.

For some schools, previous success with Paired Reading will have laid a firm foundation for further involvement with parents. Given this, the introduction of involvement in further curriculum areas based on the same principles will be relatively easy to achieve. For other schools the involvement of parents will be the primary objective in itself, and Paired Maths or Paired Science serves as a vehicle for their involvement rather than necessarily achieving a curriculum objective.

Where there are high numbers of parents whose facility with English makes Paired Reading difficult, maths games or science activities which can be discussed in detail at home in the home language offer a way of immediate involvement. Science and maths are often seen as high-status subjects meriting the involvement of a wider range of family members than is the case with literacy activities. This will, however, also raise other organisational issues, including the possible involvement of language support workers in encouraging, training and ongoing discussion.

For yet other schools, the main objective will be to raise the expectation of enjoyment and success in mathematics or science for the children and the parents. Where this is the objective, changes in attitudes will be the major focus. The organisation of the project might include 'maths club' or 'science club' badges, especially attractive games and activities, certificates for involvement and a follow-up Maths or Science party. The extra razzmatazz will affect the planning and running of both the project and its evaluation.

The issue of achievement in mathematics or science might be seen as secondary to promoting parental involvement and positive attitudes, and the project should be measured against its success in these areas. Where the achievement of increased attainment in maths or science skills is the first objective, clarifying current levels of achievement and ways of determining increased success become more necessary parts of both preparation and evaluation. Ideally all these objectives will be achieved to some measure through involvement in the project. However, determining from the outset what is the most important element will focus the organisation towards a successful outcome.

Initial consultations

Before starting the project it might be necessary or desirable to discuss its aims and practical implications with a wide range of interested parties, such as the head teacher, class teachers, Mathematics or Science Advisor or Inspector, Educational Psychologist,

Support Assistants, Parent Representatives, Governors, or School Advisors or Inspector. This period of consultation ensures that everyone is aware of what is being proposed, and has the opportunity to be involved – with the collection and preparation of the games and activities, with the day-to-day encouragement of those more closely involved, or at a more strategic level.

It will certainly be necessary to determine who has the prime responsibility for running the project: the Head, the Maths Coordinator, the Science Coordinator, the class teacher, the Special Needs Coordinator? Where does the buck stop? It will also be necessary to decide who else will be supportive in a general sense and be able to give practical support either in preparation or throughout the project.

During this initial consultation period the information about possible funding for the games or activities and equipment will need to be gathered, and means of evaluating the effects of the project will need to be decided. A small working group might prove supportive in considering all the issues. In *The Paired Maths Handbook* (Topping and Bamford 1998), Section B1 provides an organisational checklist of the issues that will need to be considered, with space for decisions to be inserted as they are made. The completed checklist can then be copied to all interested and involved parties.

Further planning – recruiting families

The pupils who are to be the focus of the project need to be carefully chosen. The objectives of the project will be the most important element in determining which pupils they might be. Where the object is to engage parents immediately on entry to the school system, the choice of pupils and parents is easy – some schools have chosen to involve their reception class children in their first few weeks in school. The expectations of the parents about their involvement in maths or science at home are thus first raised at preschool visits and the project used with all the new entrants.

For other schools where parental involvement in the curriculum has become part of a rolling programme, Paired Maths may be introduced at the start of the second term and then followed with Paired Reading in the ensuing year and/or Paired Science or Cued Spelling in the year after – or any other combination or order. Where the emphasis is on Special Needs, smaller groups of pupils may be chosen to join the Maths or Science Project in the junior school, or the Maths or Science Club in the high school. However, care to avoid any stigmatisation of the project among the peer group as 'just for slow ones' is required.

When the object is to improve achievement in maths or science, it is tempting for a first project to choose those pupils who would seem to need most help with the subject or who may benefit most. However, 'nothing succeeds like success', and long-term experience suggests that once a project has proved to be successful, it will generate more enthusiasm amongst those involved and suggest to more hesitant parents that it can be of benefit to their children. For the first project, therefore, it is important to include a good proportion of children whose parents are likely to cooperate fully – and who will be able to communicate their enthusiasm to other parents for the next time. However, take care you invite sufficiently widely, since your parent ambassadors do need credibility with the parents you most need to reach.

The number of parents likely to take up the offer of involvement in the project is a further issue to consider. You can be overwhelmed, and then be so stretched that the project cannot be run properly. If this proves to be a danger, you have to be tough-minded and prepared to say 'no' to people – while of course offering them involvement in the next project after the current one. A waiting list cultivates the desirability of involvement. On the other hand, if you are sure initial take-up will be light, you could offer the project more widely. One junior school decided to offer the project to the parents of all Year 3 pupils – 128 in all. Eventually 35 took part.

How many maths games you have available for the first Paired Maths project is critical – this will be the major determinant of how many active participants you can support at one time. Paired Science is easier because Activity Sheets can be reproduced, but there is still the question of ancillary equipment – if all the children want to do magnetism experiments at home simultaneously there could be problems! Other projects can always be arranged later. Another school offered the Paired Maths project to all the parents of the new Reception class. The parents of 11 out of the 15 children accepted. Concerns about how to support those children whose parents choose not to become involved is another issue which needs considering before the project begins – although a satisfactory resolution is often hard to find.

Where the pupils are older the project may be offered as a peer group project in school, either as part of the curriculum lesson time for all pupils, or as part of support time or lunchtime Maths or Science Clubs (see Chapter 6 – you might also find *The Peer Tutoring Handbook*, Topping 1998, useful for background reading). As after-school 'Homework Centres' or 'Supported Study Centres' become more common, Paired Maths and Paired Science will increasingly be found in them and other supplementary or alternative provision. In all cases decisions about partners will need to be addressed. Where the maths games are largely dependent on chance, the ability of one of the partners to read the instructions and to clarify the rules will be important. However, where the puzzles involve both chance and strategy, the choice of pairs will need to be more carefully teacher-directed, probably seeking partnerships including one child with greater mathematical insight. Pupils whose reading may not be fluent can sometimes intuitively solve problems by which their putatively more 'capable' friends are baffled – with interesting effects on relative self-esteem.

Regarding Paired Science, although it is nominally engineered for cross-ability pairing, the differential in scientific understanding need not be wide, and indeed *should* not be very wide if the helpers are to gain intellectually from their engagement in it, but again one partner will need to possess adequate reading comprehension skills. Paired Science sessions may be scheduled for around 30 minutes once per week in school, with cross-age peer tutors or adult volunteers, or two or three sessions of shorter duration per week at home with parents helping.

A successful project draws attention to itself – modesty does not pay. Media and public relations and marketing are worth the time invested, and can help enormously with recruitment for subsequent projects as well as the first. This often also leads to possibilities for gathering more resources at a time when these may still need to be developed.

Further preparation – project organisation

The major organisational issues are relevant to all contexts, but the time for staff to be involved in the exchange of games or Activity Sheets, and the number and variety of games and activities available, will vary depending on the number of pupils and/or parents involved.

The division of the games and activities into categories allows a choice from a different area each week, and indeed that is mandatory in the initial intensive period of operation – the six or seven week 'trial' period. The pair are given a good deal of freedom in choice of activity within an area, but pairs must take any activity *from a different area* each week. The experience of most schools is that a six- or seven-week project fits readily into half a term, so that there is no difficulty with the holiday breaks.

In order to run a Paired Maths project for six weeks for ten pupils, the minimum number of games needed is 25. This number will allow some flexibility at the weekly games exchange and will introduce at least three or four different games to choose from each week – provided you are one of the first to choose! The more pupils are involved, the more games will be needed in order to ensure sufficient flexibility of choice.

Display and cataloguing

It is helpful to have considered ways of keeping games or activities together according to the conceptual area. Coloured stickers which correspond with the conceptual area under which each game or activity is grouped are useful means of identification (see Chapter 2).

Each of the maths games will need to be labelled and placed in a plastic bag for carrying between home and school, to keep all the pieces together and as clean as possible. Paired Science Activity Sheets and any necessary equipment borrowed from school should likewise go home in a large re-sealable plastic bag. In Paired Maths, both the game and the bag need to be colour-coded to correspond with the box which contains the choice of games for the specific mathematical concept for the week. Each of the stickers can then be numbered. For example:

Ludo(Concept: Counting = red)
red sticker on box (there may be two Ludo games)
red sticker numbered '1' + red sticker numbered '2'

Scaredy Cat (Concept: Counting = red)
red sticker numbered '3' – and so on.

The colour and number coding helps with ease of exchange, and also with identification of whether any game is missing. In Paired Science, the Activity Sheets have already done much of this for you.

Exchange system

Each pupil has only one choice from each box (conceptual area) during the initial project period. The choice of game or activity needs to be recorded on the Games Loan or Activity Record Chart (see Section B5 in *The Paired Maths Handbook*, Topping and Bamford 1998, and below). Each Paired Science Activity Sheet has a code number to facilitate keeping track of who has done what, such records usually being kept by the pair themselves (see Section B4 in *The Paired Science Handbook*, Topping 1998).

Each participating child's name is listed on the chart, which is kept posted in school. The basis of the exchange is similar to a library system. Each maths game has a colour code and number, while each science activity has a letter denoting area and a number denoting specific activity. As a game or activity is chosen, it is recorded on the loan sheet under the category (colour) heading by its number. In Paired Maths with younger children, when the game is chosen an accompanying diary/language record card (also colour coded) goes home with the game. This is then returned with the game at the end of the week, the returned game is crossed out on the record sheet, and a new game chosen from a different category (colour). In Paired Science, the important scientific vocabulary is incorporated into the Activity Sheet.

For example (after two weeks):

Name	Shape (blue)	Counting (red)	Matching (green)	Strategies (orange)
Jane Smith	2		1	
Rezia Ahmed			3	1
Steven Brown		4		2

The Paired Maths Diary and Language Card Record Card monitors the time spent on the games at home and suggests appropriate language, while the overall loan chart displays where the child has sampled and where still awaits a visit, as well as providing an easy tracking mechanism for the individual games and activities.

Once the project starts, most parents are happy to do the checking in and out themselves. However there will need to be someone available at 'game exchange times' to discuss choices, oversee returns, answer questions and listen to experiences. When the game or activity chosen has proved impossible to live with for a week, some facility for 'emergency' early exchange is helpful.

Running the project – the launch meeting

Once the objectives are clear, the preparations complete and the pupils chosen, letters need to be sent out to invite the parents to come and hear about the project. With older pupils, they might create the invitations themselves. There will need to be one meeting for all the parents at the start of the project and one at the end. There are a number of issues to consider: the psychological setting, the explanation of the rationale for the project and the information that needs to be passed on.

Setting

It is best if the setting for the meeting can be informal. The experience of successful schools suggests that arranging the room so that parents can come and sit around tables with a number of games or activities ready to be used works well. Then encourage them to try out the games with each other before the explanations begin. The provision of tea or coffee at the outset helps ease this interaction. Some parents quickly get carried away – occasional enquiries about whether they can bet on the final result have been known!

The first meeting gives the parents chance to play the games or explore the activities and ask questions. Unlike Paired Reading (where children attend the launch/training meeting throughout), in Paired Maths and Paired Science the parents usually feel more comfortable and are more likely to be able to ask about issues of which they are uncertain if initially unaccompanied by their children.

The timing of the meeting is therefore an important issue. During the day working parents may be unable to come and those with preschool children may need a crèche, whereas after school parents may have difficulties with baby sitters. There will need to be some way of ensuring that the information can be given to everyone, irrespective of the different patterns of their lives and needs.

Rationale

After the first 15 minutes or so of playing the games or exploring the activities, it is necessary to talk to the whole group about the rationale of the project. The concepts underlying the games and activities are on two levels. The first is at the level of enjoyment – it is necessary to demonstrate that a mathematical or scientific activity can be both enjoyable and achievable. The second is at the level of validity – the underlying mathematical or scientific concepts need to be clear from the activity and the importance of the language made explicit. Both these underlying concepts needed to be fully explained to the parents, and related to their own experience, and you may find it more difficult with maths than with science.

An important part of the initial meeting with the parents is the opportunity to discuss the universal acceptance of the notion that 'maths is hard'. Some parents might also feel that 'science is hard'. Expect to encounter some striking gender stereotyping during the conversations, and be prepared to deal with it gently but firmly. Not many people say they like maths, and parents can easily pass a negative or defeatist attitude on to their children. However, adults often feel they are 'no good at maths' because they do not like formal 'sums' – not appreciating the wide range of different types of mathematical (and indeed scientific) activity they use in their everyday lives, in which they may in fact be perfectly competent. Parents are actually good at maths, and use maths in decorating, driving a car, baking, dressmaking, sharing things out equally, paying for purchases and budgeting, estimating journey times, and so on. Parents know more than they think! The same is true of science in everyday life. The opportunities to discuss these examples with the children can be explored.

Recent research into the differences between the mathematical achievements of children in Canada and children in Hong Kong has highlighted the difference in expectation of high achievement of the children's parents (Kwok and Lytton 1996). The launch meeting gives the opportunity to stress the importance of enjoyment and the expectation of success.

Of equal importance is the use of the games and activities as a vehicle for the exploration and understanding of the specific mathematical and scientific use of language. The discussion can help the parents to see that although the children may have grasped the everyday use of certain words, the slight change in the use of this language in a mathematical or scientific context is very important. Most children know what 'more' means when it is a question at teatime and they are being asked if they would like more chips. When the question at school is 'tell me the number that is one more than three', it is not nearly as easy to understand. Maths games (and hopefully also science activities) also have the advantage that they do not seem like 'homework' – the maths content might not be immediately visible on the surface – so children are less likely to invest energy avoiding them. The importance of the chance element in games and its equalising effect (enabling everyone to lose and reducing any danger of parents becoming more like school teachers) can also be emphasised.

This is an ideal point at which to bring the children in to the meeting. The main points can then be recapitulated and summarised (as if just for the children's benefit). Specific points at this stage in the meeting are:

- The two main aims are for the children to become more familiar with the mathematical or scientific language and feel more positive about mathematics or science.
- Parents can help their children learn more about mathematics or science through playing the games or working through the activities and talking about them.
- Mathematics is not just computation: it is learning about relationships, patterns and shapes. Similarly, science is not just about test tubes and rockets.
- Mathematics and science (like reading) is a part of everyday life. Both are relevant to everyday problem-solving.
- Maths and science can be fun!

After these points have been raised, a discussion of the games or activities is necessary. A practical demonstration of at least one of the games or activities with a clarification of the mathematical or scientific concepts and language involved is always helpful. Two members of staff might feel able to demonstrate through role play, one pretending to be the child (this always goes down well – especially with the children in the audience). During the first 15 minutes while the parents are playing the games and exploring the activities, the members of staff will have been able to talk with the parents individually and any questions or issues raised at that time can be included in the general discussion.

Information – practical details

It is necessary to clarify what the commitments are for both the parents and for the school staff. These are:

For the parents:

- take part in the project for a limited period (e.g. six or seven weeks),
- play a game or do the activity chosen by them from those provided by the school for a minimum of 5 to 10 minutes and a maximum of 20 minutes,
- use the language on the Diary Card or in the Activity Sheet as much as possible,
- complete a Diary Card and return it to school each week (for maths). For science, families sometimes write directly on the Activity Sheet.
- exchange the game or activity each week for another one (from a different box or conceptual area in the first six or seven weeks),
- attend a further parents' meeting at the end of the project.

For the school staff:

- supply the mathematical games or Activity Sheets and more technical equipment,
- operate the game/activity library exchange,
- be available to discuss and help as necessary,
- arrange a further parents' meeting at the end of the project to plan for the future.

The families need to be told where the games/activities will be kept, what days and times are scheduled for game/activity exchange, who the key people are in school to ask for help and advice, and how to record which games/activities have been borrowed.

Looking ahead – trouble-shooting

It is important that the parents themselves come into school to change the games/activities, to ensure access to ongoing support and encouragement, but some special arrangements may need to be made where this is not possible.

It needs to be stressed to the parents that 20 minutes should be a maximum in order to avoid over-exposure to the games and resulting boredom. They may need to think of ways of shortening potentially long sessions, e.g. stop when the first person gets to . . . The Record Cards give space to say how long the games have been played for. Paired Science activities quite often occur in fewer but longer bursts of concentration. It is helpful to check when the games/activities are returned and to talk to parents who may be being over-enthusiastic (or children who are wearing out their parents).

It is also necessary to point out that, on occasion, the children may become bored with a particular game or activity before the week is over. In this case, either a different game or activity can be devised from the one that is available, or a different game/activity used which may already be available at home, or an early exchange with school could be arranged. It is unlikely to happen but it is necessary to know what to do if it does. Parents may also need advice about playing games and carrying out activities at different levels, progressing to using games/activities in new and various ways, using other games/activities at home, and relating the mathematical and scientific language in the games to mathematical and scientific language used in 'real-life' applications.

Telling the parents what to do when the dog chews up a vital piece or the baby leaves interesting stains on the game is very important. The parents need to know that the most important point is to let the school know about damaged or missing pieces, so that they can be replaced. The 'no blame' policy needs to be made clear to ensure that taking part is the most important thing – some wear and tear is inevitable. Ways of fund-raising or a working group to oversee mending or replacing are both options to support maintenance and/or restocking.

The mathematical and scientific words provided on the Record Cards and emboldened on the Activity Sheets need to be used, and the time spent is an opportunity for parents to use this language with their children to ensure that they are clear about the meaning. It is therefore usually necessary for the parents themselves to play the games with their children rather than leaving it to a sibling (although it varies with different siblings). If the other members of the family want to play, it may be worth finding a different time and a different game or activity that can include everyone. However, experience suggests that part of the value of Paired Maths and Science for the participating target child is that it legitimises obtaining some positive individual attention from one or other parent, so siblings pushing their noses in might not necessarily be welcome – it depends on the specific culture and sociology of the family in question.

Towards the end of the meeting, ask if there are any remaining questions. Once these have been dealt with (but not before), add that any other questions people think of can be discussed individually at the end of the meeting (some parents will be very reluctant to ask their question in a large group setting). At the end of the meeting, a leaflet should be given to the family which reminds them of the main points that have been discussed (for Paired Maths, see Sections B2 and B3 in *The Paired Maths Handbook*, Topping and Bamford 1998; for Science, see Section B1 in *The Paired Science Handbook*, Topping 1998). These parent leaflets can also serve as part of the 'script' for a slightly nervous teacher conducting their first launch meeting. Do not however give out the leaflets early in the meeting, as reading will interfere with listening.

Rounding off the meeting

When all the practical details have been discussed, the parents can be asked to choose a game or activity to take home for the first week. At the end of the meeting, the parents should have:

- a game or activity plus equipment,
- for Paired Maths, a Record Card with the appropriate words for the particular game,
- an explanatory leaflet,
- a date for the follow-up meeting,
- details of the exchange (with whom and when).

Sometimes a badge for the participant children taking part is made available. (Sometimes parents want one as well!) This helps promote group bonding and mutual excitation and support, and also makes the badge wearers a walking advertisement for future projects.

Before the parents leave, the system of recording should be used to record their choice of game or activity.

The follow-up meeting

This serves a number of functions:

- exchange of feedback between parents and teachers,
- evaluation of the project,
- further planning.

For the exchange of feedback, the meeting should be more open and relaxed, without the children. Sitting in a circle, with tea or coffee provided, helps the discussion to be more informal. Getting some sort of feedback or evaluation from the children beforehand (either on tape or through questionnaires) is a way of giving the parents the children's views and prompting a discussion of the parents' and teachers' viewpoints. Try to bring in the quieter parents and avoid domination of the meeting by the vocal – be they parents or teachers! The leader of the discussion will need to have a number of possible points or questions already in mind so that all the issues are covered, e.g. ease of taking part, appropriateness of the games or activities, particular favourites (this usually elicits some funny stories), good things to celebrate, problems to address for next time, and so on.

Evaluation of the project

The parents' comments on maths Diary Record Cards or science Activity Sheets will already have given valuable information, a distillation of which will be appropriate to share with the parents at the meeting. The feedback session will also provide the opportunity for exchanging a great deal of information about the positive effects and about any problems that were encountered. As soon as the parents arrive they could be asked to complete a Parent Evaluation Questionnaire (see Section B7 in *The Paired Maths Handbook*, Topping and Bamford 1998, or Section B7 in *The Paired Science Handbook*, Topping 1998), which will help them to focus on some of the questions under consideration and which will provide further formal results for future planning.

Future planning

Many parents and children may well wish the project to continue in some form, albeit less intensively. Each family or set of partners should feel able to make whatever choice seems right for them – and of course reserve the right to change their mind. If they wish to continue after the trial period, they have complete free choice across all areas, and can pursue their own current enthusiasms. Of course this means that in any week, most pairs will be doing a different activity from other pairs. Thus any formal discussion and review in class is even less feasible, although as children informally discuss their experiences and begin to recommend activities to each other, some interchange does spontaneously occur.

The meeting needs to be a celebration of all the commitment and continuing involvement that has been shown. Certificates for the children or rosettes for their badges can be a part of the celebration. For the parents a pocket book of ideas for further maths games or science activities could be given as a 'thank you' offering and stimulus to continue.

For some schools the whole meeting becomes a celebration of maths or science, with further activities available for the parents to see and to try, some school-curriculum-related, others home-oriented. For other schools, especially where the parents have home languages that are not English, the next potential project group of parents is invited to come and hear the experiences of the parents who have been involved, so that they can talk together about what it was like. This capitalises on the modelling effect and marketing power of enthusiastic participant parents, whose influence in reassuring and encouraging potential recruits is enormous.

The follow-up meeting also provides the opportunity to discuss with parents other proposals from the school or to ask the parents for suggestions, e.g. having a games or activities library in school, forming a parent (and teacher) group to make more games or activities, or raising money to fund further projects. Ideas may be put forward that will lead to further involvement. Once parents have had their own self-esteem boosted, know they are valued by the school and see specifically how they can help, they can be a very powerful force for their children's learning.

Particularly in schools with no tradition or history of parental involvement, the first project might meet with only a limited or rather lukewarm response. Don't worry. This is not unusual in communities where families have learnt to see the school as an institution and teachers as authority figures who blame parents rather than helping them. Families do not automatically trust schools – that trust has to be earned. Once your first project has been successful (as it must be), the word will begin to spread through the community. More parents will become interested, and an increasing proportion of them will be parents you had considered difficult or hard to reach. As you persist, continuing to organise well and avoiding over-reaching yourself and compromising the quality of implementation, eventually a critical mass of interest will develop, and the project will take on a life and energy of its own. After that, your main problem might be keeping it from growing so large that it is completely out of control!

CHAPTER 4

Research findings in Paired Maths and Science

This chapter is in two sections. Section A briefly reviews the research literature on educational practices and developments related to Paired Maths but not the same, under five subheadings: maths games in class, cooperative learning in maths, peer tutoring in maths, parental involvement in maths in North America, and parental involvement in maths in the UK. Much of this also has implications for Paired Science, other projects related to which are then discussed.

Section B reports evaluation research on the effectiveness of Paired Maths itself in more detail, particularly that involving parents (Chapter 6 includes evaluation of a peer Paired Maths project). The chapter concludes with a summary of research to date specifically on the Paired Science programme.

Section A

Maths games in class

The use of maths games in class is now considered a mainstream activity, recommended in the National Curriculum in England and the 5–14 Mathematics Curriculum in Scotland. Indeed, games and puzzles were mentioned as 'required' resources in the Mathematics 5–14 Curriculum, which specifically recommended board games and number and shape puzzles and advised that games should cater for a range of abilities and interests in a class, including pupils with special educational needs.

Previously, the Cockcroft Report (1982) had recommended the use of enjoyable mathematical puzzles and problems, presenting mathematics as a subject 'to use and to enjoy', in order to promote confidence in applying mathematical ideas. However, what is meant by a game can vary greatly. 'Games' used in classrooms by teachers often prove to be two dimensional, mechanistic and tightly focused on 'school numeracy' (often number operations) – little more than interactive worksheets – and certainly very different from Paired Maths games.

Perhaps the major argument for mathematical games is that children and adults have always enjoyed playing them. Such games have been around for thousands of years and have been discovered by archeologists. In Orkney, rudimentary stone playing pieces and Viking boards marked in a grid have been found, chess pieces were discovered on the Isle of Lewis, and games dating back to far more ancient civilisations have been found in China and Egypt.

Beasley (1990) suggested four classes of games in mathematics: games of pure chance, games of mixed chance and skill, games of pure skill and automatic games. He added that if games were dependent only on skill, the results would be predictable and the games might soon lose their appeal. As well as emphasising the chance and fun aspect, Cornelius and Parr (1991) asserted that there were many mathematical issues inherent in good games, waiting to be drawn out by the perceptive teacher. Thus children should be encouraged to discuss the games and carry out investigations in which they might develop their own strategies for success and variations of the games themselves. This could be followed by a brief written and/or graphical account of the investigation with a comment on the game and perhaps their own written version of the rules, circulated for the benefit of other children.

Several books on the use of mathematical games in education have been published, e.g. Hughes (1986) and Skemp (1989a,b). Hughes (1986) saw mathematical games as an ideal way of stimulating and motivating young children and suggested that games provided both meaningful contexts and meaningful translation between the concrete and the symbolic. Skemp (1989a,b) described how children could work in pairs or small groups, creating the conditions for cooperative learning. He also suggested that mathematical games could be a useful stimulus for talking about mathematics. In the context of games, children could express their ideas freely and receive feedback, cognitive challenge and correction from their peers in a non-threatening way.

Work in the area had already been going on for some time (e.g. Burrett 1968, Skemp 1971). Dean (1978) reported a study of the use of mathematical games in the primary school, with pupils with mathematical difficulties on a small group basis. He noted that some games promoted the use of mathematical language while others did not. A short-term gain in mathematical ability was found, but few details are given and it is not stated whether any measurement was undertaken in the longer term.

Hughes (1983) introduced two groups of four-year-old preschool children to a rudimentary form of arithmetical symbolism using simple games. All the middle-class group and half of the working-class group achieved some understanding of numerals and operational symbols through the games, but there was limited spontaneous generalisation to other contexts.

A wider discussion of games in mathematics learning was offered by Rogers and Miller (1984), emphasising their value in embodying mathematics within concrete and palpable referents as recommended with young children by Piaget, Bruner, Dewey and others, as well as their motivational power and the value of the extra practice in promoting consolidation and transfer. Using number games with high school pupils aged 12 and 16 and also primary school pupils aged 9, Rogers and Miller (1984) applied a criterion-referenced pre-test and post-test of mathematical ability, and also intermediate and follow-up tests, including tests of generalisation. Test performance improved and this was sustained at follow-up. There was also evidence of transfer of

45

effects. However, findings would have been strengthened by the inclusion of a traditional control group.

Subsequently, McConkey and McEvoy (1986) described the use of games with children with severe learning difficulties, many of whom do not find it easy to learn to count. Numeracy had often been accorded low priority in special schools for such children. Working with children and young people aged 11 to 18, these authors emphasised the value of games in terms of enjoyment, purposefulness and attendant meaningfulness, all leading towards functionally effective simplification of the counting process. Spontaneous learning through modelling was considered a potent element, as was the 'safety' of the game environment. Pre-tests and post-tests were conducted with participants and control students. The latter showed no change, while the games group showed change which was highly statistically significant, evident over the whole ability range. Later, the games proved equally effective in the home setting.

Maths games were also used with children with disabilities by George and Mosley (1988). Children involved included those with partial sight and blindness (for whom games in Braille were available) and with hearing difficulties (grouping to ensure that communication was feasible proving essential), as well as those with physical and learning difficulties. The value of the games for 'overlearning' was noted, and older children were comfortable engaging with mathematical content at an appropriately low developmental level in a game in a way they might well not have been in formal instruction. Unfortunately no evaluation was reported.

In summary, there is accumulating evidence of improving quality concerning the effectiveness of games in aiding mathematical learning, even with children with many and severe learning difficulties.

Cooperative learning in maths

There is a substantial literature on cooperative learning of mathematics, but hard evaluation is less common and very few of the studies used games, although games were sometimes a small part of a larger programme of activity.

Davidson has provided several reviews of research on small group cooperative learning in mathematics (Davidson 1985, 1989; Davidson and Kroll 1991) and a handbook of readings for teachers (Davidson 1990). He mentioned the following common features:

- division of the class into two- to six-member groups,
- group discussion of maths concepts,
- group practice of techniques,
- group solving of maths problems,
- teacher monitoring and managing of group process,
- teacher checking of work and assisting where necessary.

He asserted that cooperative learning of mathematics was useful with all age and ability levels and all curriculum topics, including in higher and adult basic education.

Individual accountability and team recognition should be inbuilt.

Forming groups heterogeneous in ability is usual, and support for this also comes from Webb (1985, 1991) and Askew and Wiliam (1995). Webb (1985) suggested that mixed-ability grouping facilitated access to peer explanations and was positively correlated with achievement. Johnson and Johnson (1991) also supported hetero-geneous groups in terms of attainment, and teacher-assigned rather than friendship pairs. However, for reciprocal peer tutoring, similar attainment levels might be more appropriate. Same-sex pairs seem to be most popular among the children. Girls were reported by Wood and O'Malley (1996) to fare less well in mixed dyads than in same-sex pairs.

Gains from cooperative learning in general are reported by Slavin (1990) to include positive effects on achievement, self-esteem, time on task, liking of class and classmates, and cooperativeness. However, not all studies have found these positive outcomes. Specifically in mathematics, Davidson (1985) suggested that these were only consistently found for computational skills, simple concepts and application problems.

Davidson and Kroll (1991) reported that less than half the studies in mathematics showed significant differences in student achievement between cooperative and traditional methods. Those which did showed the small group method to be more effective, and the authors suggested that the giving of explanations in small groups was positively related to student achievement. It was not clear whether cooperative learning with or without rewards was more successful.

Pratt and Moesner (1990) compared traditional instruction and cooperative learning with low ability 11-year-olds. The cooperative learning class performed better on tests of language, reading and mathematics, although only the latter reached statistical significance. Urion (1992) found small-group learning as effective as teacher-directed instruction in high school and college mathematics classes, with some evidence of better long-term retention for the former. Reid (1992) compared the mathematics test achievements of 13-year-olds *post hoc* according to whether they had experienced co-operative learning or individualised/competitive instruction, finding differences reaching statistical significance in favour of the cooperative learning group. Nichols and Hall (1995) examined the application of the Student Teams Achievement Divisions model of cooperative learning to geometry learning among 16-year-olds. Significant gains compared to traditional instruction were found on a variety of test parameters. Other relevant and interesting reports have come from Slavin (1985), Mevarech (1985), Kyriacou (1991), Duren (1992) and Nattiv (1994).

In the UK, Askew and Wiliam's (1995) review of the research asserted that cooperative work did have positive effects on pupil achievement in mathematics, although the data were not open to detailed scrutiny.

Topping (1992) acknowledged that there could be some disadvantages in cooperative learning. These included a considerable investment in planning and set-up time, and also difficulties with quality control. A dominant child in a group could cause others to take a passive role and create a 'free rider' effect (Mulryan 1992). A dysfunctional division of labour and an over-emphasis on competition might result in destructive conflict (Johnson and Johnson 1991).

In summary, there is a good deal of evidence that cooperative learning in mathematics can be effective in aiding mathematical learning, perhaps especially in certain domains of mathematics, but that good results are by no means automatic. This might imply that good quality planning, organisation and quality control are necessary to ensure positive outcomes.

Peer tutoring in maths

As with cooperative learning, there is a substantial literature on peer tutoring of mathematics, but although hard evaluation is somewhat more common in this field, the use of games is still rare.

The effectiveness of peer tutoring in general has been widely acknowledged for many years, as various reviews and meta-analyses have indicated (Sharpley and Sharpley 1981, Cohen et al. 1982, Topping 1988, Topping and Ehly 1998). Britz and his colleagues (1989) reviewed the effects of peer tutoring specifically on mathematics performance. After examining studies from 1980 to 1989, it was concluded that peer tutoring was effective in promoting significant cognitive gains in mathematics for both tutors and tutees, including with populations of low-achieving, mildly handicapped or socially disadvantaged children.

Same-age peer tutoring in mathematics with eight behaviourally disordered middle school tutors and tutees was found by Franca and colleagues (1990) to result in improvement in maths scores and attitudes towards maths for both, as well as significantly improved social interactions. Charles Greenwood's Classwide Peer Tutoring (CWPT) model has resulted in longitudinal improvements in mathematics achievement for at-risk participants as well as in other curriculum areas (Greenwood 1991). John Fantuzzo's Reciprocal Peer Tutoring (RPT) model, involving alternating roles between partners, was found to improve the mathematics achievement of 64 academically at-risk students aged 9 to 11 (Fantuzzo et al. 1992). Adding group reward to the structured peer tutoring further increased effectiveness. Phillips and his co-workers (1993) combined class-wide curriculum-based measurement and peer tutoring in 40 primary (elementary) mathematics classes. Results indicated that students of low and average previous achievement (including those with learning disabilities) achieved significantly better results than students in control classrooms.

The effects of previous training and experience in peer tutoring of mathematics operations on its outcomes were studied by Fuchs et al. (1994) in 16 primary (elementary) school classes. Partners with experience and training in a step-by-step verbal feedback routine provided more interactional explanations and incorporated sounder instructional principles, although in both conditions, student explanations tended to be algorithmic rather than conceptual. Subsequently, Bentz and Fuchs (1996) investigated the effects of providing training and practice in helping behaviours during peer tutoring in mathematics of 7- to 9-year-old students with learning disabilities. Students who received the helping training engaged in an increased number of directly trained helping behaviours than the untrained students.

In Scotland, a cross-age peer tutoring project in a primary school has been reported

(Renwick, personal communication). Pupils aged 11 each tutored two to three younger (age 7–8) pupils, using materials closely articulated with the school mathematics curriculum. Video process data was gathered and the tutors were asked orally what they thought about the project, but no summative evaluation is reported.

Fantuzzo and his colleagues have also considered the additive effects of peer and parent tutoring in mathematics. Working with 84 10- to 11-year-olds, Heller and Fantuzzo (1993) found that students who received reciprocal peer tutoring (RPT) plus parental involvement (PI) showed higher levels of accurate mathematics computations than those receiving peer tutoring only, who in turn scored higher than control students. Fantuzzo *et al.* (1995) then replicated this with 72 urban at-risk 10- to 11-year-olds evidencing difficulties in mathematics, finding that students who received PI + RPT displayed higher levels of accurate mathematics computations on a curriculum-based measure than PI or control students, and had significantly higher scores on a standardised measure of mathematics computation than control students.

In summary, peer tutoring in mathematics has been shown to yield significant achievement gains on both criterion and norm-referenced mathematics tests, and gains in attitudes to mathematics, self-concept and social interaction, especially with at-risk and low achieving children. Gains for both tutors and tutees are evident. Gains are more likely to be substantial with training and experience for participants. Extending to also include parental involvement appears to have a further additive effect.

Parental involvement in maths in North America

Although a substantial number of projects have been reported, finding hard evaluative evidence is more difficult. The Cognitive Enrichment Network (COGNET 1991) Follow Through project involved teachers, parents and preschool and primary grade children in a wide range of activities at home and school. Children experiencing two years of intervention did better than control children on norm-referenced reading and maths tests, and also on cognitive tasks and a measure of intrinsic motivation. Parents reported improved problem-solving and increased enthusiasm for computer use in their children, and felt their own confidence had improved. However, the impact of the individual strands of this multiple programme were not separately evaluated.

In Canada, Onslow (1992) reported an evaluation of the Family Math programme in Ontario, involving 149 parents and their 9- to 10-year-old children. There was evidence of improved attitudes to mathematics in both parents and children, and increases in the parents' understanding of current methods of teaching mathematics. However, no evidence of increased attainment in the children was given.

The 'Natural Math' programme was a family involvement project for preschool and kindergarten childhood mathematics undertaken with Head Start African American children and children of the Oklahoma Seminole tribe of native Americans, seeking to integrate mathematics within the family's own culture and needs (Sears and Medearis 1992). Maths activities and games were suggested, materials provided (including for use during the summer vacation), and a portable computer lab made available. With the African American group, the Natural Math materials were introduced to the children before they were given to parents. Participating children showed higher verbal and maths post-test scores than children from the previous year, but exact comparability between years was not established.

A more satisfactory research design was employed by Brodsky and his colleagues (1994) in a controlled evaluation of two successive years of a short series of Family Math programmes. Measures were taken of child and parent attitudes towards mathematics, child achievement in mathematics, and teacher behaviour. In the first year there were 101 experimental and 89 control children; in the second, 211 experimental and 234 control. Only two of the analyses showed statistical significance. Experimental children with prior Family Math experience showed higher gains on standardised mathematics performance measures than other groups. Family Math parents showed increased general involvement with their children's schools. The parents were very positive about the programme but reported no significant increase in confidence for themselves or their children. Participating teachers were likewise very enthusiastic.

In summary, evaluative evidence on parental involvement in maths in north America is somewhat mixed in quality and outcomes, and less than conclusive. While attitudes to maths may improve and other spin-off benefits be found, parent and teacher enthusiasm for, and appreciation of, a programme is not necessarily coupled with hard evidence of attainment gain. It may be that longer involvement is necessary to yield measurable attainment gains.

Parental involvement in maths in the UK

A small but ambitious arithmetic project involving the parents of high school pupils whose mathematics development was delayed was reported by Jennings (1983). Six participating families and a self-selected comparison group were pre- and post-tested using a norm-referenced number test. Work was prepared in school for the children and supplemented with number games. Parents were required to attend weekly contact meetings in school. The experimental and comparison group had almost identical scores at pre-test. After five months, the experimental group had made the equivalent of 12 months' progress on the test, while the comparison group made only four months' progress. Many of the experimental parents had underestimated their child's difficulties and all felt their child's confidence had increased. The project meant the experimental children did not have to be withdrawn for specialist tuition, which might have been stigmatising and damaged their self-esteem and/or peer relationships.

Another interesting small study (Woolgar 1986) used individualised objectives-based programmes for the six 7- to 8-year-old children involved, who were taught at home by their parents for five weeks using a scripted direct instruction method-ology. A comparison group matched by age, gender distribution and pre-test scores on a norm-referenced number test was formed. Criterion-referenced placement tests were also used to determine the starting point for each individual programme. Weekly contact meetings with parents to evaluate and develop the individual programmes took place. At post-test, on the curriculum-based measurement the experimental group had gained 12 points while the comparison group gained only one point. On the norm-referenced test, the experimental gain was higher than the comparison group gain, but this difference did not reach statistical significance – perhaps unsurprising with such small numbers. Subjective feedback from parents and children was generally positive.

Seventeen children with difficulties in mathematics from seven different primary (elementary) schools were involved in a ten-week project reported by Perry and Simmons (1987). Parents and children made their own choice of a maths activity each week, which included some games, puzzles, problems and investigations. Norm-referenced pre-test scores also gave diagnostic indications of priority areas for different children. The importance of enjoyment, discussion and praise was emphasised. Minimal materials were required other than a calculator. Three of the 17 children dropped out. At post-test the remainder showed a statistically significant increase in mathematics quotient – their achievement had increased more than expected of 'ordinary' children during that time. More fathers were involved in the maths project than had been involved with the same children in a previous reading project. Subjective feedback from parents was positive and all but two wished to continue.

Seven primary school pupils experiencing difficulty with mathematics were involved in a ten-week maths projects based on games described by Clive (1989). Again, discussion, praise, and regular short periods set aside at home for the purpose were integral. Home–school contact was sustained through a diary system. Participant children gained on a norm-referenced test administered before and after the project, but the significance of this is not given and no comparison group was used. As ever, subjective feedback was very positive and improved attitudes to maths widely reported.

Neilan and Currie (1994) involved parents in a series of four workshops over a six-week period, involving mathematical workbook tasks and problem-solving activities which were continued at home and supplemented with number games. Pre- and post-norm-referenced number tests were applied to children in a mixed ability class of 18 5-year-olds randomly assigned to control and experimental groups. Uptake was 100 per cent and attendance at workshops very good. The control group was offered involvement in the programme after post-test. Experimental and control parents were asked not to confer! In the event, the experimental and control groups were not equivalent on pre-test scores, those of the latter being lower. Experimentals gained more on the test than a comparison group, but the difference did not reach statistical significance. Subjective feedback from parents was very positive.

In summary, a number of small and brief projects in the UK have nevertheless shown encouraging results, especially as three were controlled studies. Children involved ranged from very young primary school children to high school pupils, mostly but not exclusively those with mathematics difficulties. Gains have been demonstrated on various kinds of tests although not all gains reached statistical significance – this being elusive with small samples. Subjective feedback was ubiquitously positive. The time costs to parents of involvement varied greatly in different projects, and this has implications for the wider involvement of more parents.

Overall, then, there are strong indications that maths games, cooperative learning in maths, peer tutoring in maths and parental involvement in maths can all be effective separately. The Paired Maths method seeks to blend selected elements of these approaches together into a robust and dynamic package. In Section B evaluation research on the effectiveness of Paired Maths itself is reported in more detail, particularly that involving parents. Chapter 6 includes details of evaluation of peer Paired Maths projects.

Other projects related to Paired Science

A number of initiatives to promote parental involvement and peer tutoring in science have developed in recent years. In the UK, the School Home Investigations in Primary Science (SHIPS) project was modelled upon the long-standing IMPACT maths approach. The SHIPS team noted that much existing science material had an unthinking 'recipe' approach to yield the 'right' answer, and were concerned to devise activities which could be approached in a number of different ways (Solomon and Lee 1991). Following IMPACT methodology, the expectation was that each half term the class teacher would prepare all the children for the same activity, which they (hopefully) carried out in the same week at home with their parents. This clearly maximises curriculum linkage and the opportunities for subsequent whole-class discussion and review of everyone's experiences. However, it could seem rather too much like old-fashioned 'homework'.

A team of community educators in Humberside County Council produced a 'Parental Involvement in Science' pack (Chambers et al. 1992), which deliberately sets out to emphasise the 'fun' element in science. It includes tasks such as 'design and build a shelter into which four members of the family can fit, using only newspaper and sellotape' and 'devise a test to see what kind of carrier bag is the best'. The number of activities outlined is not large, as the intention is to lead teachers into creating their own ideas. The linkage to the curriculum is perhaps less obvious than in the SHIPS approach, but the motivational power seems likely to be high. The materials are illustrated with cartoons and there is discussion of the social management of introductory meetings with parents.

Similar developments were occurring elsewhere in the world. The Great Explorations in Math and Science (GEMS) programme in the USA produced a Parent's Guide to GEMS in 1991. The US Government offered a publication titled 'Math, Science, and Your Daughter: What Can Parents Do? (Campbell 1992). The American Chemical Society's Education Division created the Parents and Children for Terrific Science (PACTS) programme. Rillero (1994) reviewed the emerging field. In Australia, Science PACT (based on the maths IMPACT programme in the UK) developed (search the Internet for current website).

However, no evaluations of any of these programmes or materials seem to have been published as yet.

Section B

Evaluation of Paired Maths in Kirklees

Evaluation research on the effectiveness of Paired Maths in the family setting was undertaken in three stages: the evaluation of the pilot project, the evaluation of the subsequent supported projects, and the in-built evaluation of those projects which became part of the ongoing parental involvement in the schools.

Evaluation of the pilot project

The initial Multiply Attainments Through Home Support (MATHS) project was devised as a joint home–school project, building on the experiences of the parental involvement projects within the Kirklees Education Service in West Yorkshire, England. The main aim of this project was to explore whether a home-based maths project would have similar positive effects to those already obtained through home reading. Initially the project was aimed at a target group of 7-year-olds, as this was considered to be the age by which expectations as to a certain degree of numeracy would have been formed.

Setting up the pilot project

The pilot infant school was an urban school with a wide-ranging population. The staff had already been considering ways in which to involve parents in the education of their children and they were very willing to direct efforts toward the numeracy of a small group of pupils.

New parents were invited to take part in the project. These were the parents of children who were in the top age group (age range 6 to 7) and who were thought likely to benefit from help with number at home. Seven out of nine parents agreed to be involved, there were three girls and four boys. A meeting was held after the project to ask for the parents' reactions.

What parents and children thought
Information about the parents' views was obtained through the meeting, through discussions with the teachers, by means of an evaluative questionnaire completed at the end of the eight-week project and through a follow-up questionnaire six months later. All the parents were able to continue with the daily maths session most of the time throughout the project. They also kept records as suggested. The majority found it easy to take part in the project and the instructions easy to follow. Except for one parent, there were also no difficulties in using the words as prescribed on the language cards. In all cases, their children would sometimes remind the parents when they forgot about the daily session.

The time spent by the parents and children on the activities was on average about 15 minutes per session, but some parents regularly spent as much as 30 to 45 minutes a day. There was no evidence of a tail-off effect in the majority of families. Most parents, though, admitted to having been bored sometimes, or to their children having been bored. This appeared to be related to the specific activity chosen, rather than the overall length of time they had spent on the project. The activities that were preferred most were activities that were more like a game involving some competition. These were also more clearly recognisable to the parents as number games. The other activities were criticised mainly in terms of being too difficult or too inflexible. Some parents had also created or added their own games, although this was not as frequent as the project leaders had hoped.

Most parents said they would probably carry on doing maths games with their children, but not every day. They felt that the project could be improved by providing more interesting games. They mentioned specifically board games, card games and other counting games as possibilities. Most felt that their children had enjoyed taking part and had benefited from the project. Except for one parent who found it difficult to do the project and frequently became bored, all parents said they would recommend the project to other parents.

Six months later, five out of seven parents returned the follow-up questionnaire. These suggested that they were all continuing to play maths games with their children at least once a week, with two parents doing this three to four times a week. Their children asked them from time to time to do maths games, and most children were reported as having become more interested in maths since being involved with the project.

Teachers' views
The teachers were asked to complete a checklist and an evaluation sheet on the children in the project. In addition various discussions were held with the teaching staff throughout the project.

The class teacher did not find it difficult to arrange meetings with the parents for a brief discussion and an exchange of games. In six of the pupils, positive changes were noted in classwork, while some had also improved in their behaviour or in their relationship with their teacher. Of course, these changes could not be definitely attributed to the project, as there are many factors which could have been involved. However, the teachers felt that the children benefited from individual assistance, even if it was not obvious at first, and that the project improved the children's attitude and motivation.

Another reason for welcoming the help given to the children was that it had not been possible to provide all the individual tuition which they thought desirable for their pupils in class, and the project allowed some assistance with this. The involvement with parents was thought to be particularly beneficial. One question raised was whether the project should have continued for a longer period of time. Generally, the teaching staff had enjoyed taking part in the project.

Pupil assessment
Assessment via pre- and post-project testing, which had been widely used in evaluating home reading projects (Topping 1995), was used as a model. All the pupils in the class were tested on both the Young Mathematics and Young Reading group tests

before and after the project, with a seven-month gap between testings. However, a group test of mathematics was found to be very limited and problematic with such young children, and the results showed wide variation. Four of the five tested pupils increased their scores and 'maths age', two of the pupils by 11 months. One showed no test gain at all.

While it was possible that these results reflected to some extent the progress made in developing mathematical skills, their accuracy was questionable, particularly because of the wide divergence in the scores. Even more divergence was found using the test with the whole class group of 28 pupils, their gains ranging from +17 months to -6 months. The fluctuation in the reading scores of the whole group was far less than in the maths ages and they were all positive. However, on individual test items concerned with elements of language and pattern, the project group differed from the rest of the class. Both pattern and language had been emphasised in the project, and had been mentioned by the parents as an area in which they had noticed change in their children.

It was concluded that this group method of testing for change in mathematical knowledge was too insensitive to give a clear picture of the effect of such a short-term intervention.

Establishing the Paired Maths approach

Subsequent to the pilot project, a further four experimental projects, two with infant reception children (aged 4 to 5) and two with first year juniors (aged 7 to 8), were operated. The experience of these projects and the reactions of parents, teachers and children suggested that similar positive effects to those already outlined with home reading could be achieved with maths through this approach. Each of the projects followed basically the same format as the pilot, but with two important extensions that had been suggested by the pilot evaluation. The first was a greater variety of games to choose from, which could therefore be changed weekly. The other was a greater emphasis that the time spent should be enjoyable and not exceed 10 to 15 minutes a day.

Following the initial pilot project each subsequent project built on the experiences of the previous ones, and attempted to explore or develop some aspect of the parent involvement or the evaluation (for a more detailed description of the format of the projects see Chapter 3).

The numbers of children involved were:

Infant (6–7 years) pilot project: 9 children, 2 teachers

Infant reception (4–5 years) projects:
Project 1 – 9 children, 2 teachers
Project 2 – 19 children, 3 teachers

Junior first year (7–8 years) projects:
Project 1 – 9 children, 1 teacher
Project 2 – 29 children, 4 teachers.

Quantitative evaluation

Measuring changes in the children's mathematical knowledge before and after the intervention was clearly problematic. Individual rather than group assessment seemed likely to be more reliable, and various types of measuring instruments were available:

(a) norm-referenced tests,
(b) criterion-referenced tests,
(c) observation schedules,
(d) interview schedules.

Commercially-published norm-referenced tests often covered a wide range of ages and mathematical operations, and were not found to be nearly sensitive enough to be used to determine individual progress in specific areas. Criterion-referenced tests were often too time-consuming for teachers to use (this was before the introduction of National Curriculum assessments) and also too narrow in the range of mathematical concepts that were involved. Observation and interview schedules, although often sufficiently illuminative, were again inevitably time-consuming. These difficulties had been noted in the Cockcroft Report (1982):

> any test which is given to a child can measure performance only on that part of what he has learned to which the test questions relate; even then, he may not always be able to demonstrate his knowledge under test conditions.

In the second infant project, all the parents for the new intake for that term were invited to take part. Twelve of the 16 parents took up the offer. The children in the next term's intake, who were not offered any project involvement, were used as a comparison group.

An alternative method of providing some measure of any changes in mathematical learning was necessary. After much exploration and discussion, the Quest diagnostic tests (Robertson *et al.* 1983) were used as the basis of individual interviews, which were held with all the experimental children pre- and post-project, and with the comparison children over the same time interval.

The children were tested individually during their second week in school, with activities exploring their concepts of Pattern, Shape, Sorting, Conservation and Ordering. The same tests were then repeated after eight weeks, so some practice effect could be expected in both groups.

The project children showed a marked improvement, particularly in the areas of Pattern, Ordering and Conservation. The children in the comparison group, although showing some improvement in their scores, scored significantly less well than the project children, particularly in these same areas. Pre-project scores for project children were on average below those of the comparison children, but post-project this situation was reversed (see Figures 4.1, 4.2 and 4.3).

The school was so pleased with the ease of managing the project and with the effects on the parents and the children that they instigated a further project with the next year's intake, and subsequently adopted the approach alongside Paired Reading for all entrants in ensuing years.

Projects with 7 to 8-year-olds
Before the start of the junior school projects a major effort was launched into further analysis of the games which would be needed and into the provision of a broader range of games. Professor Richard Skemp from Warwick University was invited to extend the discussion, and various ways of funding the new games were explored.

The greatest difference between the infant and junior projects was the ease of joint involvement for parents and teachers in the infant school in the exchange of games. In the infant school the parents were already visiting school to collect their children, but in the first junior school project the parents' main contact was through the home–school record card. In the second junior project this distancing was reduced by explicitly contracting for the parents to visit school weekly to exchange games with the children, and for the teachers to be available to discuss aspects of the games where necessary.

Subsequent evaluation proved this to be an important aspect of the project, as was the pre-project meeting without the children where the parents were given the opportunity to play and experiment with the games before involving the children. This pre-project meeting was used as a forum to stress the need for recognising that although the children may have grasped the everyday use of certain words, the slight change in the use of this language in a mathematical context was very important.

Qualitative evaluation
Evaluation of each of the projects involved not only the children but also the parents and the teachers. Parents were involved through discussion at meetings before and after the project, discussion with teachers, the completion of record cards and

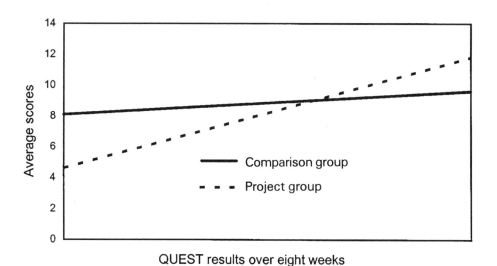

Figure 4.1 Pre- and post-test total scores on QUEST test

Pre/post test for project group

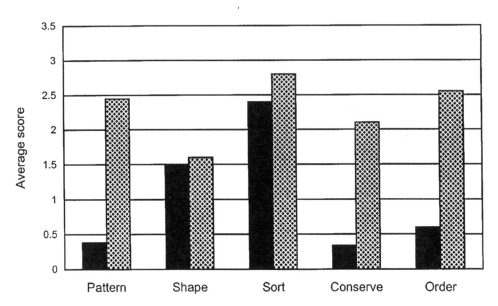

Figure 4.2 Pre- and post-test sub-test scores on QUEST

Comparison group results

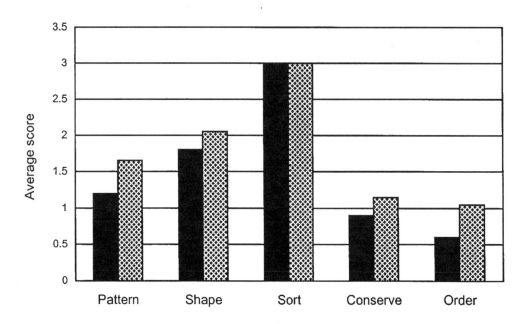

Figure 4.3 Pre- and post-test sub-test scores on QUEST

questionnaire returns after the project. Teachers were involved through discussion at meetings and on other occasions during, before and after the project. Pupils were involved through parents' observations and questionnaire comments, observations by teachers, and tape-recorded discussions after the project.

Together this feedback, albeit subjective, gave a more complete evaluation of the project. The parents' reactions were very positive and suggested that they had found it easy to take part in the projects. The introduction and use of the mathematical language generally presented no problems. They reported that the children were sufficiently keen to play the games that they would remind their parents if they forgot, and only occasionally did either parents or children become bored with the activities. Many of the parents said that the games had given them ideas of other things to do at home and that they would continue to play games even after the project was finished.

Both the parents and the teachers felt that the children's confidence in maths had increased, and both remarked upon the children's disappointment when the project ended. In maths projects, unlike reading projects, there is no public library or other ready source of further materials toward which participants can be directed. However, the parents had a wealth of ideas on how the project could be extended. One group suggested meeting together to make games that could then form the basis of a 'maths library' kept in school, while others suggested a 'swap shop' of mathematical games. Perhaps the best evaluative indicator was the enormous enthusiasm and impetus for the project to continue.

Further developments

Subsequently, many more schools showed interest in developing parental involvement in mathematics, including schools for children with learning difficulties. Meanwhile in Kirklees, the Paired Reading Project extended its brief to all curricular areas and was renamed The Paired Learning Project. Under this umbrella, more support services could be offered to schools wishing to develop projects. Handbooks were produced for extra-district enquirers, and there was very favourable publicity in the national press resulting in the distribution of well over 1,600 manuals worldwide. The contents of The Infant Games Kits were revised, and separate loan kits were produced for Junior Schools. Subsequently, Games Kits for High Schools were compiled, especially suitable for peer as well as parent tutoring.

Follow-up evaluation

Since the initial establishment of the Paired Maths approach, seventeen schools have been visited and interviews held with the head teachers and teachers involved in the continuing parental involvement in maths. All of the schools continued to rely on the subjective feedback evaluation given by the parents and children through their verbal and written comments and their continuing involvement in the project.

Six of the schools had incorporated Paired Maths into their annual cycle of parental involvement alongside Paired Reading. The numbers of pupils generally involved included the whole year group, operating at different times during the year – extending to many hundreds of children in any one of the schools over a period of years.

One of the schools with a large proportion of children for whom English was not their home language had made the Paired Maths their premier way of involving new pupils and their parents, who could use their home language to play the games and their contact through the language support tutors to explain to and encourage their children. For some such families, the high status of maths and science perhaps gives more motivation than would be found in a project focusing directly and only on language development.

In each of the schools where the project was an embedded part of the parental involvement, the organisation had become much more the responsibility of the parents themselves. The continuity of the project was seen as a success from this point of view, as well as from the more obvious gains in increasingly positive attitude towards maths.

Paired Science: summary of research to date

To date, evaluation of Paired Science has only been through participant feedback, from questionnaires and group meetings with parents and teachers in schools. Results from three Paired Science projects in different parts of the UK have been reported (for more detail, see *The Paired Science Handbook*, Topping 1998).

The Shaw Cross Project
All 26 children in a class of 6-year-olds (Year 1) participated in a seven-week project, and a feedback questionnaire was completed by every family. Parents were extremely positive about their children's reaction to the Paired Science activities, almost all reporting seeing more interest in and enjoyment of science in their children. Almost as high a proportion of children appeared to show cognitive gains in understanding and communicating scientific ideas and applying scientific methods. In two-thirds of cases the children seemed more confident about scientific matters and were generalising their curiosity to a wider range of issues beyond those in the Pack.

Also highly encouraging was the very positive view of the impact upon the parents' enjoyment and understanding. Amongst continuation options, going on with Paired Science occasionally was by far the most popular. Half as many parents intended to stop and half as many intended to continue doing science at home but without using the Pack. These positive indications were reinforced by the additional written comments on the questionnaire and the verbal comments made by parents in the feedback meetings.

The Millers Neuk Project
In a P4 class of 28 7 to 8 year olds, 26 chose to participate, two of whom dropped out of the project owing to domestic difficulties. All the remaining 24 families returned a questionnaire, referring to 8 boys and 16 girls.

Verbal feedback was collected from parents, and also children and the volunteer 'science library' helpers. Again, parents were generally positive about their children's reaction to the Paired Science activities, two-thirds or more reporting seeing more interest in and enjoyment of science in their children, together with increased understanding and an increase in questioning about everyday phenomena. A majority of children were felt to have benefited under every possible evaluative heading, although only half had definitely improved their ability to give better explanations – possibly because short-term changes in children of this age are not so striking as in younger children. A substantial majority of parents felt they had benefited themselves.

A significant majority of parents indicated they intended to continue with weekly activities, and only three (10 per cent) reported an intention to stop science activities at home. The questionnaire results were also analysed by gender groups. Parents of girls were more likely to be 'unsure' about observed changes in the children than were parents of boys, by a factor of 50 per cent. Unequivocal improvements were thus reported in a higher proportion of the (smaller number of) boys, especially with respect to interest, enjoyment, improved explanations and increased general questioning. In contrast, the parents of the girls reported much greater gains for *themselves* in enjoyment and understanding than did the parents of the boys.

Classroom observation indicated that the children were more interested and confident in science in class and were better at testing out ideas practically. There was evidence of generalisation into practical investigations in science classwork. In the classroom the girls appeared less confident in science than the boys.

The Broom Nursery Project
This interesting experiment in extending the Paired Science methodology to four-year-old children in a nursery school also yielded encouraging results, despite taking place in the rather short and disrupted summer term ending in a long holiday. Twenty nine parents participated, of whom 27 returned the evaluation feedback questionnaire (93 per cent response rate).

Almost all parents reported increased enjoyment in science in their children, three-quarters increased questioning about science, and well over half observable gains in competence and confidence in science. Parents were also very positive about what *they* had gained from the project in understanding and enjoyment.

Many parents expressed surprise at the capabilities of their child and were pleased at the increased questioning. Some parents reported an impact on reading, with children increasingly likely to seek out science books. However, the question was raised of whether the children might be required to repeat similar experiences in the first year of primary school, as many of their peers might not have had the Paired Science experience, and there was concern about discontinuity and the possibility of failure to capitalise on the early advancement demonstrated by the participant children. Of course, they could be excellent same-age peer tutors for their less fortunate classmates!

Even the quiet children developed the confidence to experiment and investigate, and there was some generalisation into class of the more able helping the less able. Children were seen to ask more intelligent questions in class, and certainly increased their use of the embedded scientific language. The coordinating teacher concluded 'the science activities stimulate imagination and promote a feeling of awe and wonder, while allowing children to begin to control their own environment'.

CHAPTER 5

How to evaluate Paired Maths and Science

This chapter looks at different ways of evaluating your own Paired Maths or Science Project. The issues involved in both quantitative and qualitative assessment are discussed. We will not dwell here on issues of research design, which readers can explore elsewhere (e.g. Topping 1988). A main focus will be on problems of assessment and measurement in mathematics (and science by implication), particularly with young children. For subjective participant feedback, examples of questionnaires which have been used with both pupils and parents are provided in *The Paired Maths Handbook* (Topping and Bamford 1998) Sections B7–B10, and in *The Paired Science Handbook* (Topping 1998) Section B7.

The most important question to ask at the beginning of any discussion of appropriate evaluation is: what was the purpose or objective of the project – what was the desired outcome? The next question concerns how you intend to measure whether the objectives or outcomes have been attained, and this will lead you to consider qualitative measures, quantitative measures, or both.

Qualitative evaluation

The term 'qualitative research' is often used to describe any kind of research that yields findings not arrived at by means of numerical or statistical procedures. Some of the information may however still be quantified (for example, the number of parents who said that they found it easy to take part in the project), so there is no definite boundary between quantitative and qualitative methods. Additionally, both methods can be used together to illuminate reality in different ways – there is no real conflict between them.

When the analysis is predominantly qualitative, there will however usually be an attempt to use a wide range of information to uncover the details of the project which are most important in making a difference. Qualitative methods are more likely to have what is sometimes called an 'eductive' or exploratory approach – less concerned with exact data on precise but possibly rather artificial instruments, and more concerned with interpreting the meaning and significance of everything which actually happened. Qualitative evaluation often relies on the subjective experiences of the people who are involved with the project. The emphasis is placed on understanding and trying to determine the value of the involvement from the experience and attitudes of those taking part.

Where the purpose of the project is to involve parents in the learning experiences of their child and the parents who are invited actually take part throughout the project, then the very fact of their involvement constitutes a positive evaluation. Further evaluation can be gained through discussion and questionnaires, to refine the nature of the parents' involvement and gain information on how to make it more inclusive or more rewarding. Testing of the children's achievement would not be necessary if the objective of the project was merely to involve parents in their children's learning.

On the other hand, if there is a need to evaluate whether the children have in fact been learning, or learning more, it might be necessary to test whether or not any learning has taken place. However, clarification of what sort of learning is intended by the project needs to be defined in order to make the evaluation meaningful. If the purpose of the project is to increase the children's confidence and positive attitude towards maths or science, an individual measure covering items that have not been addressed by the project will be unlikely to provide a positive outcome in terms of test scores. A more appropriate evaluation would be gained by either open discussion, or by questionnaires for the children looking for evidence of attitude change, supported by observations or questionnaires from both parents and teachers.

Whenever questions are asked there is always the possibility of biasing the answers by the way they are asked. Judd *et al.* (1991) noted that attitude questionnaires, which focus on subjective phenomena, were difficult to write because attitudes tended to be complex and multi-dimensional. The attitudes expressed by respondents depended upon a complex interplay of factors such as the wording of the question, the question sequence and interviewer effects. The level of specificity of the questions was also significant: general and specific questions might produce different answers, with specific questions likely to elicit information with higher validity. Examples of questionnaires which have been used with both pupils and parents are provided in *The Paired Maths Handbook* (Topping and Bamford 1998) Sections B7–B10, and in *The Paired Science Handbook* (Topping 1998) Section B7.

The most important aspect of the qualitative approach is to determine what information you really want. The questionnaires need to express the questions in the most straightforward language and with the minimum of written response for parents or children who would find this daunting, while giving the opportunity to provide extended information to others who may wish to do so.

While a Paired Maths project is running, there is the opportunity for ongoing evaluation from the parents on the Diary Record Cards which are returned weekly. From these you can determine the average length of time spent on the project at home, the number of times each week that the games were played, and the parents and children's views of the individual games. All this information can add to your evaluation of the project, whether you analyse it formally or not. It will also provide you with insight into those families for whom written responses are not easy – where further evaluation may need to be in the form of a discussion rather than a written response.

Obtaining valid qualitative feedback from the children might be particularly difficult, especially if the children are young and/or have limited communication skills, and 'teacher' is asking. Leutzinger *et al.* (1993) suggested cooperative problem-solving and peer evaluation as part of the assessment process in mathematics. Other methods of assessment suggested by Beyer (1993) included observations and reflection. Where Paired Maths projects have involved pupils in peer group work, the questionnaires in Section B9 and B10 in *The Paired Maths Handbook* (Topping and Bamford 1998) have been used.

Quantitative evaluation

By contrast, quantitative methods are more often associated with a 'deductive' or confirmatory approach – the researcher has a theory about what might happen and sets out to prove or disprove it. Of course, the value of a deductive approach depends on the researcher having a useful and sensible theory in the first place! Many teachers conducting action research find themselves using mostly qualitative methods at first, perhaps adding 'some quantitative methods later when they are clearer about what would be useful to try to measure more precisely and objectively, or what theory they wish to specifically test.

Quantitative research is the term used to describe the use of numerical or statistical data, especially to determine whether any differences between sets of data or results are significant, with implications for what is causing what. In an experimental situation where everything else remains the same or equal, a statistically-significant difference in the end result can be attributed to the effect of the one element that was varied. Being able to ensure that there was only one possible varied element, one possible cause for any difference, is not easy in the complex real world environment. That is why, where statistical differences are used, group results are often compared to minimise the impact of great individual differences between children.

Quantitative evaluation therefore refers to evaluation which can provide numerical data to support an objective view of the outcomes of the project. In a Paired Reading project, for example, these results may be provided by the change in the scores of a reading test given before and after the project. The measurement of achievement in maths has however proved to be even less straightforward than with reading. Group maths tests have been designed, and would therefore seem to be useful if given before and after a Paired Maths project. However, they tend to be very wide-ranging, as maths is such a vast subject and mathematical competence far from being a unitary skill.

Additionally, the complexity of the understanding of symbols getting in the way of showing an understanding of the concepts provides an immediate barrier to easy assessment. Needless to say, science tests are rarer and even more problematic – although they rely somewhat less on symbolic knowledge, they tend to rely even more on diagrammatic information.

Where the initial objective of the project is increased observable mathematical or scientific understanding, here again specific and clear objectives are necessary in order to lead to a sufficiently sensitive instrument for evaluation. Where the emphasis is placed on the understanding of precise mathematical language, the test needs to be directed towards identifying such increased understanding. Where the emphasis is upon being able to work with the underlying mathematical concepts, the test needs to be directed towards assessing increased meaningful learning. Especially with young children, an individual approach may be the only way sensitive enough to explore any changes in an individual's understanding. Any attempt at assessment through writing immediately requires the abstract symbolism of either words or figures, which then comes between a child's understanding of a problem and their expression of a solution.

The selection of a measuring instrument to provide quantitative evaluation depends on the purpose underlying the decision to test, and whether group or individual administration is practical. The age, range of ability and attainment of the children also affect the choice of test. The difficulties of identifying a suitable test in relation to the purposes of the project and the nature of the sample need careful consideration.

Three types of instruments are available:

1.   norm-referenced tests,
2.   criterion-referenced tests,
3.   diagnostic interview/observation schedules and kits.

All of these have their difficulties. The first group (norm-referenced tests) focus on finding out how many of a selection of mathematical or scientific tasks pupils can and cannot do, and are rarely sensitive enough to be used to determine individual progress in specific areas. The second group (criterion-referenced tests) are very time-consuming for the teachers and too insensitive to changes in how children learn. In England, the National Curriculum Standardised Attainment Tasks are a form of criterion-referenced testing, which however many educators have found to be rather cumbersome, inefficient, imprecise and inconsistently applied between different teachers. The third group (diagnostic kits) are potentially sufficiently illuminative, although mostly available only for mathematics. However, their use on an individual level is again inevitably time consuming:

> any test which is given to a child can measure performance only on that part of what he has learned to which the test questions relate; even then, he may not always be able to demonstrate his knowledge under test conditions (Cockcroft Report 1982).

Cockcroft (1982) emphasised that tests 'should enable candidates to demonstrate what they know and should not undermine the confidence of those who attempt them'. On the positive side, Orton and Frobisher (1996) suggested that tests might provide information that teachers did not already possess, arguing that assessment could provide early insight into children's difficulties and misconceptions. This view was supported by Askew and Wiliam's (1995) review of research in mathematics which suggested that pupils learn more when their teachers know their current level of attainment and can act on this information.

Norm-referenced maths achievement tests

These often focus on numerical operations, especially arithmetic – which is only a small part of mathematics. The individual's score is interpreted by comparing it with scores obtained by many others on the same test. They offer little diagnostic information. Depending on their design and the size and representativeness of the normative sample, they can have good reliability and superficial validity, but because of the width of the skills covered they are unlikely to be sensitive to small but important changes in understanding.

Examples of such normative tests are the 'Group Mathematics Tests' by D. Young (published by Hodder and Stoughton), which are designed for use across the full ability range with Year 2 infants and Year 3 children (i.e. 6–7-year-olds). They also have norms for older pupils. They focus particularly on basic arithmetical processes and also set out to assess a wide range of mathematical understanding and skills at a simple level, using two parallel forms to help control for practice effects. Another example is the 'Staffordshire Mathematics Test' (published by NFER-Nelson), a group test for children aged 7–8, which claims also to 'identify specific areas of difficulty'. Sixteen such specific areas are mentioned, but as the whole test has only 64 questions, each diagnostic area is assessed by only three questions.

In the USA, a parallel example would be 'The Stanford Diagnostic Tests', intended for students aged 6 to 18 – but the coverage is wholly number and computation. The 'Test of Mathematical Abilities' (TOMA-2) attempts to be broader, covering computation and story problems but also mathematical vocabulary, attitude to maths and 'application to real life' – but only for ages 9–18. For younger children, the individually-administered 'Test of Early Mathematics Ability' (TEMA-2) claims applicability to children aged 3 through 9, but again is tightly focused on computation.

Criterion-referenced achievement tests

These are intended to determine whether or not a child has acquired a clearly specified skill measured in a specific way. They may be produced by teachers in relation to their own curriculum objectives, to assess the degree of mastery pupils have reached on a topic. Their advantage is that they can be designed to assess the programme that has actually been taught, rather than one that might have been taught – in other words, they have high 'ecological validity' and make sense to the key players in the real world of their own classroom. They do not have to be age-related. However, if they are individually designed they will need moderating if they are to be used more widely, in order to establish whether they can be applied equally to other children and other teachers. Criterion-referenced tests can subsequently have norms attached and be used at national level.

One example of a criterion referenced maths test is the CATCH criterion-referenced screening battery for children aged 6½ to 8½ (final year infants/first year junior) (from the Godfrey Thomson Unit for Educational Research, University of Edinburgh). This battery is mainly intended to identify children with difficulty – in other words, for screening purposes. There are many easy questions – the test has a long discriminatory 'tail'. It is available in equivalent forms A and B, and sub-tests include 'The Language of Early Mathematics and Mathematical Procedures'.

Another example is 'Assessment Activities in Mathematics', by Aileen Duncan and Lindsay Mitchell (Faculty of Education, University of Strathclyde [formerly Jordanhill College], Southbrae Drive, Glasgow G13 1PP. ISBN 1 85098 099 3). Intended for ages 3 to 7, this comprehensive battery of 450 items covers number, time, weight, length, volume, money, area and shape. Standard concrete materials are not provided but listed for each item, while more exotic materials are provided.

Maths diagnostic interview/observation kits

Working in detail with individuals allows for more careful investigation of what the children are able to understand. Several instruments have been designed to investigate aspects of the maths curriculum in further detail. 'The Basic Number Diagnostic Test' by Bill Gillham (published by Hodder and Stoughton), is designed for individual use with children in the age range 5 to 7, and covers the basic number skills 'that a child might reasonably be expected to have mastered by the age of 7 years'. However, for a project where a variety of mathematical concepts are being covered along with the mathematical language closely connected with those concepts, more wide ranging instruments need to be used.

For example, The QUEST Screening, Diagnostic and Remediation Kit has been used successfully to explore the development and acceleration of early mathematical concepts in Paired Maths projects (see Chapter 4). The children were tested individually with activities exploring their concepts of Pattern, Shape, Sorting, Conservation and Ordering. The second edition of Quest (by Alistair Robertson, Ann Robertson, Joanna Fisher, Anne Henderson and Mike Gibson) is now available from NFER-Nelson. It is designed for children aged 6 to 8 and is said to be usable on a group basis also.

'The Early Mathematics Diagnostic Kit' (developed in Tyneside/ Northumberland by David and Margaret Lumb) is also available from NFER-Nelson. This has a collection of test items for 4 to 8-year-olds and older children with learning difficulties, taking about 30 minutes per child. The intention is to help identify difficulties and select, implement and monitor teaching programmes. The Kit covers number, length, money, shape, weight, time, representation, and capacity – all of which are defined in terms of behavioural objectives. There are 110 test items in all. Unifix cubes and boxes are used in some items.

'Early Mathematics Concepts' by John Ashby, Graham Ruddock and Steve Sizmur (from NFER-Nelson) claims to enable assessing 4 to 5-year-olds in small groups as well as individually, taking 15 to 30 minutes per administration. As with some of the instruments mentioned earlier, EMC can serve diagnostic and baseline assessment functions, and inform subsequent teaching strategies. The items profess to measure what mathematical knowledge children bring to school, rather than what they have learned in their early months in school, and claim to be useful for children who have English as a second language or who have special needs, but users will need to inspect the test items to satisfy themselves about cultural and community relevance for their own catchment area.

In the USA, a similar approach was taken by *The Sequential Assessment of Maths Inventories* (SAMI) by F. K. Reiseman. This has been available in the US since 1985, and more recently in UK through The Psychological Corporation (24–28 Oval Road, London NW1 7DX). It has a wider age range (5–13). Individually administered, it covers mathematical language, ordinality, number and notation, computation, measurement, geometric concepts, mathematical applications, and word problems. It provides some norm-referenced comparisons as well as diagnostic information.

Process evaluation and interpreting outcomes

If you specified your desired objectives or outcomes for your Paired Maths or Science project, applied measures to find out whether they were achieved, and had a disappointing outcome, think carefully about why this might have been:

- Were your objectives too wide-ranging or unrealistically high?
- Did you measure only the outcomes *you* wanted to see, forgetting that other key players might have had quite different objectives, which were not measured?
- Was the project organisation appropriate in theory, but just not properly implemented (for whatever reasons), so your results are not a fair test of the programme when properly implemented?

You need to be gathering information about the quality of programme implementation as you go along in any case, since even if you get good outcome results, you might be able to see points at which things could be made even better. Also, if the programme was very poorly implemented, and you still get very good results, you will want to consider whether this is miraculous or whether there are artefacts in your measuring procedures which are producing apparent gains where none really exist (e.g. via practice effects, questionnaire construction bias, and so on). If on the other hand your programme was well implemented, but did not yield positive results, you need to ask yourself about the measuring instruments used – were they relevant or sensitive enough? Or was it that the programme design was perfectly appropriate for some cultural settings and contexts, but not really for the one in which you operate?

In short, poor outcome results might be the result of wrong objectives, wrong organisational planning, poor implementation, wrong measures, or some combination of these. If you suffer from any of these, take steps to fix the problem – you will need some good luck as well, but do not rely on it.

Reliability, validity and evaluation

Because of their content-specific nature and the fact that they may be designed for a particular group studying a topic in one school, criterion-referenced tests are less likely to have high broad-spectrum reliability and validity than norm-referenced tests. Equally, individual diagnostic assessment is very specific to the individual on an individual occasion. However if the same experience is given to all the children that are included in the assessment, the group results can give some indication of possible areas of difference.

Reliability refers to the consistency of scores obtained on a measure, for example when the same subjects are assessed with the same test on different occasions. The questions should have been so carefully devised that there is confidence in the correlation of alternate forms given to two sets of pupils at the same time. Also, the scoring system should be so clear that there can be confidence that any two different scorers would give the same mark, providing scorer reliability. Validity, on the other hand, is concerned with what the test actually measures and how well it does it.

Evaluation is the process of determining whether the project has been successful in its aims and whether the effort involved has been worthwhile. It cannot be over-emphasised that in order to appropriately evaluate any intervention the most important aims of the project need to be identified from the start. Many of the schools who have decided to make a Paired Maths project part of their ongoing work with parents have chosen not to evaluate beyond the weekly record card of the parents and the spontaneous response of the teachers and children involved. Their aim has been to increase parental involvement and they have been content that the project has provided an appropriate vehicle for this to happen.

Evaluation is not an end in itself, nor necessarily a 'good thing' by definition. Teachers need to consider why they are conducting an evaluation – the evaluation itself should have its own purposes and objectives. Evaluation costs time, effort and money, and time spent evaluating is time not spent doing other things – there is an opportunity cost. Teachers should thus be clear and honest (not least with themselves) about what they hope to get out of evaluation and what it is worthwhile putting in to achieve that.

Evaluation methods specific to Paired Science

The Paired Science materials are designed so that evaluation is interwoven with the activities (see Section B6 in *The Paired Science Handbook*, Topping 1998). It goes without saying that the effect of Paired Science should show up in National Curriculum assessments. However, teachers might wish to evaluate Paired Science more precisely and efficiently than this.

Apart from the obvious evaluative evidence contained in the stored completed Activity Sheets, the children and helpers will be happy to give their views in a group feedback meeting, whether separately or together. There will be many hilarious stories of experiments gone wrong and what was learned from the disaster! However, not everyone is extrovert. Asking the helpers to fill in the simple evaluative questionnaire provided (see Section B7 in *The Paired Science Handbook*, Topping 1998) enables everyone's opinion to be noted. This is a single sheet with ten questions and multiple-choice answers, quickly completed and even quicker to check and summarise. It provides a cost-effective and quotable index of consumer satisfaction.

From the helper's point of view, the development of a more positive attitude to science is also important, and ways of accessing this should be considered by evaluators. A parent will only communicate a positive attitude to science if they themselves feel clear about what they are doing, feel supported by the school and are involved in activities which are interesting and entertaining in their own right. Most helpers at home will probably be mothers – many of whom might have a poor self-image of themselves as scientists. By giving them a structure in which they can succeed as science tutors, not only might their own scientific knowledge be revised and possibly added to, but their own view of themselves and their attitude to science might improve considerably. These benefits should then advantage other younger children in the family in due course. Similar benefits can accrue to older children who act as Paired Science tutors in school. However, attitudes are notoriously problematic to measure with any reliability or validity.

Obviously, day-to-day classroom observations also offer much insight into the value of the Paired Science activities, as children are seen to grow in confidence and increasingly are able to generalise their knowledge. (Some of the questionnaire items could be used as an observational checklist.) How much of this growth is attributable specifically to Paired Science will be difficult to tease out, unless an acceptable means of involving only half the class at a time has been found, so the relative progress of participants and non-participants can be compared.

Assessing changes in scientific understanding is made much easier by the scientific 'key word' structure. Through the whole 45 activities, ten key words occur very frequently and a further 70 occur more than once. Children's understanding of a random sample of ten high-frequency key words could be checked before starting Paired Science and their understanding of a different random sample of ten after Paired Science.

More sophisticated evaluation of Paired Science is necessary, and the next step here is to use the keyword scientific vocabulary structure built into the pack to assess improvements in understanding and usage of these concepts, preferably on a pre-post-test basis and using a non-participant control group. Beyond this there is a need to assess maintenance of any such gains at longer term follow-up. There is also a need to assess generalisation of enhanced skills (as distinct from knowledge), but pre- and post-skill generalisation tests would require detailed and time-consuming observation and sustaining the reliability of the procedure could prove a problem.

Also much needed is exploration of differential effects with different gender groups and different gender matchings in tutorial pairings. Further exploration with other age groups and with populations in areas of greater socio-economic disadvantage is also necessary. With any intervention there is the danger of giving further advantage to those who are already advantaged.

CHAPTER 6

Cooperative learning and peer tutoring in the maths classroom

This chapter examines the use of Paired Maths in a peer tutoring and cooperative learning context within a primary school. It describes the intervention and the effects on the children's attitudes to mathematics, on their self-esteem, on their attitudes to working cooperatively and on their performance in a mathematics test. The reflective practitioner will draw much from this report which could also be applied to cross-ability peer tutored Paired Science projects, in addition to the guidance on organisation already provided in Chapter three of this book.

Previous work

Detailed feedback from participants in a same age peer Paired Maths Level 3 project involving parallel classes of 11 to 12-year-olds in a high school in a disadvantaged area was collated by Topping and Bamford (1990). Preferred games were Labyrinth and Pass the Pigs, followed by Yahtzee, Uno and 5 in a Row. No box of games was considered uninteresting, but the strategy box was generally considered the most interesting. The number of games provided was thought adequate, but duplicate copies of the most popular were requested. Three-dimensional commercially-produced games were preferred to two-dimensional locally-produced games. However, the instructions were considered too long and too hard for several games, especially the commercial ones. Despite this, the participants saw little need for an ability differential in the pairing – perhaps meaning mathematical rather than reading ability. No difficulties in organising activities with partners was reported. No participant became bored – a change of game easily avoided any such possibility. Discussion about how to play the game was commonly reported; pairs sometimes agreed to change the rules, especially if the original instructions were very complex.

Overall, participants definitely found Paired Maths both interesting and fun. They felt a majority of the games made them think harder. However, they were unsure about whether they liked 'maths' any more – although they certainly liked the maths games! Thus their highly positive attitude to the games containing maths had not been perceived to generalise automatically to the formal school maths curriculum. A few participants felt they could do 'problems' better in formal maths classes, and there was spontaneous comment that needing to read complex instructions very carefully improved the ability to do this in other subjects. A few felt they could now design their own maths games. Virtually all would recommend Paired Maths to other people. Improvements to the system could include duplication of the most popular games, improving instructions, including more solitaire puzzles, having longer sessions, building in the switching of partners and providing solutions to 'impossible' puzzles.

The vast majority of participants wished to go on doing Paired Maths. Verbatim comments included: 'it didn't feel like maths, because it was fun' and 'it was not proper maths, but it WAS thinking and problem-solving'. The participants seemed to continue to espouse a very narrow definition of 'proper' (i.e. schooled) 'maths', equating it almost entirely with number. Thus only Paired Maths number games (e.g. Equality, card games) were cited as definitely improving ability in 'traditional' maths. Of course, these subjective perceptions might not reveal the whole truth.

Somewhat similar projects had been reported elsewhere in the secondary sector, run by a learning support teacher and a mathematics teacher (Carmichael 1995, personal communication). Maths games were initially used in peer tutoring of low-attaining first and second year high school pupils (aged 11 to 13) by able 16 to 18-year-old students for three 15-minute sessions per week over four to six weeks. Subsequent projects paired third year (13 to 14-year-olds) average ability tutors with first year tutees. However, no evaluation details were reported.

An approach with some similarities was reported by Neumark (1997) at a multicultural secondary school for girls in London, here as a three-week 'strategy project' embedded annually in the curriculum to help develop analytic thinking (as required by the 'using and applying maths' category of the English National Curriculum). After exposure to a number of games from different countries, the pupils were required to devise their own game and explain it to the rest of the class. Again, evaluation was only anecdotal.

Context and sample

The project school was a large city primary school in Scotland, with a roll of 512 and three forms of entry, staffed by 26 teachers, two of them full-time learning support teachers. It catered for a mixed population, many of whom came from single-parent families, and some social deprivation was reported. Interest and priorities within the school at the time of the project were focusing on discipline and improving cooperation and behaviour on a whole-school basis. The formal mathematics curriculum was strongly conditioned by the National Curriculum guidelines for 5–14 years laid down by the Scottish Office, akin to (but less rigid than) the 'National' Curriculum in England and Wales.

The experimental group was a mixed ability class of 25 10-year-old children (P6 in Scotland, the penultimate primary class). The comparison group was a parallel class of 20 children, who did not play the games but received normal mathematical instruction from their teachers. The mean ages of the classes were very similar, but other differences were perceived by the teachers. The experimental class was seen to have some social, emotional and behavioural difficulties and a large group of middle to low attaining pupils. The children were described as having poor social skills, not forming a very cohesive group and often falling out with each other. The school felt these children could benefit socially from the maths games project. The comparison group was reported to have a more harmonious social grouping and a wider range of ability. The experimental class had a male teacher who appeared to have a good relationship with his pupils. The comparison group had two female teachers in a job share.

Preparation

A timetable was agreed – the project was to run in the spring term. However, the amount of time needed to set up a first project from scratch should not be underestimated. Games need to be gathered, categorised and coded, and rules and instructions simplified.

The school agreed to obtain 20 to 25 games, by using some from existing stock and buying some new ones, but generally concentrating on number skills. The researcher gathered the others, for loan to the school. Games suppliers proved difficult to locate. A number of stores reported that they no longer stocked games and puzzles which would have been suitable for the intervention. The best games and puzzles were found in certain stores and toyshops in the run-up to Christmas. Another difficulty is that games cannot be played before buying, making it difficult to ascertain what will be suitable. Gathering the games took two to three months. A few spare replacement counters and dice were also purchased.

The mathematical content of the overall pool of games and puzzles was considered in relation to the 5–14 curriculum guidelines. Then each was allotted to one of four categories:

1. Shape, Position and Movement,
2. Number and Money,
3. Strategy and Logic,
4. Puzzles.

Games could be played by two or more players, while puzzles presented a problem for one person. These categories were similar to those used in the original 'Junior' Key Stage 2 kit, but it was decided not to use the fifth category of extension games for mathematically-able pupils, since there was little indication of who the mathematically-able might be and the researcher was reluctant to make assumptions about both children's ability and the relative difficulty of the games and puzzles.

The games and puzzles were then colour-coded and labelled: blue for Shape, yellow for Number, red for Strategy, white for Puzzles. Where puzzles were too small to label in this way, the puzzle box or bag was labelled instead, together with an indication of the number of pieces for that puzzle. This was to enable a child putting the puzzle away to see easily if pieces were missing. Some puzzles and games were put into zip-up plastic bags so that pieces were less likely to get lost. Categorisation was difficult, as Cornelius and Parr (1991) also observed. Whether a game fitted better into the Strategy or the Shape, Position and Movement category was hard to assess. This could have been a focus of discussion with the children. Labelling was adequate but the games would perhaps have been better numbered 1 to 80, so that the children did not have to record the games by their number and their colour category.

The researcher played most of the games and solved most of the puzzles provided by herself. This was time-consuming but essential. She then simplified rules and rewrote instructions for the majority of these. However, the school did not have the time to try out their games or simplify rules. In the end there were too many games and puzzles for such a short intervention: 80 in all, when 50 would have been adequate. For the class of 25, to allow a little choice, around 16 to 20 games and puzzles were needed for each session. Storage space for the games was limited, and this could make changing games and accessing different categories problematic.

Procedure

The project was a short one. The children played the games for two 30-minute sessions each week for six weeks, and wrote brief comments about the games in notebooks at the end of each session. The experimental group generally played the games in pairs, although there was often also one group of three. Children doing puzzles worked largely individually, and this provided the change of pace recommended by Johnson and Johnson (1991).

The children had been put into pairs and one of four groups by the class teacher. Pairs were organised so that there was one child who could read well in each pair, to facilitate the reading of the game instructions. This had the additional advantage of providing a heterogeneous ability mix in each pair. Girls were generally put with girls rather than in mixed dyads. Each of the four groups of six children (one had seven) was initially allotted one of the four categories of games and puzzles:

1. Number and Money;
2. Shape, Position and Movement;
3. Strategy;
4. Puzzles.

These categories then rotated round the groups at the end of each week.

Monitors in each group collected their group's games at the start of each session and checked that they had been tidied up at the end. Small jotters were provided to each child in the experimental group. In these they wrote the date, the name and category of the game they played, a short comment about the game and a rating out of 10. These notebooks provided additional process evaluation on the project.

The first games session was run by the researcher and the class teacher. A sheet of written instructions about how the sessions would operate was available for each pair.

These were used for instruction and as a reminder in the first two games sessions but became superfluous as a routine was established. Each group monitor then collected the games for their group and each pair chose a game (for the puzzles each child chose an individual puzzle). The game or puzzle was recorded in the child's notebook, the instructions were read and then the game was played.

The adults circulated around the groups while they were playing, encouraging and helping some confused pairs to follow their game instructions. Towards the end of the session the teacher instructed the pairs to add up their scores and put away the games. A further five minutes was allowed for writing a comment in their jotters. This routine was adhered to at all the games sessions, sometimes followed by discussion between the class teacher, the researcher and the children about the games and any difficulties or successes which they had experienced.

Measures and assessment

Despite the brevity of the intervention, it was decided to use a mathematics test to see if there was any measurable impact on performance. However, administering an individual test would be too time-consuming with two classes totalling 49 children, so a 30 to 40-minute group test was required. This should not be so difficult as to discourage the children (Cockcroft 1982), and it should cater for a wide spread of ability so as to minimise ceiling or floor effects. Published norm-referenced tests were either too difficult or too easy, or the range of attainment covered was too narrow, or the reading requirement was too high for the children in the sample. A further disadvantage was that they were likely to be too insensitive to register differences in attainment over a six-week intervention.

A criterion-referenced test was therefore devised by the researcher which was more appropriate for the age, ability and interest range of the children in the sample. This had the additional advantage that questions could be selected which related to the mathematical areas and vocabulary of the games. Unfortunately there was no time to pilot the test before the start of the project. Although it appeared to have face validity, other types of validity were indeterminate.

The test devised consisted of 30 questions. Fifteen questions in Section A were designed to assess the children's understanding of mathematical words. Most of these were multiple-choice questions, but in some cases the children had to respond in a different manner, e.g. by drawing a counter on a grid. The 15 questions in Section B were concerned with number and money operations and line symmetry. The selection of questions did not attempt to cover all the Mathematics 5–14 strands, because not all of these were reflected in the games used during the project, and constructing appropriate questions was easier in the areas of number and money than in shape, position and movement and problem-solving.

Each question was read out by the researcher to help the weaker readers and to allow time for the children to think about the question. A short amount of time was then allowed for them to write down their answer. The researcher started to read out the next question when it was clear that the majority of the children were ready. The test took about 30 minutes to complete.

An attitude questionnaire was also devised by the researcher, containing statements relevant to attitudes to: mathematics, self-esteem and working cooperatively. A Likert scale was utilised for all items, ranging from 4 (high positivity) to 1 (low positivity). Scoring yielded a total score and sub-scores in the three domains. Again, piloting proved impossible. The questionnaire consisted of 16 statements: 8 reflecting positive attitudes and 8 negative attitudes. Five were concerned with attitudes to mathematics, 6 with working cooperatively and 5 with self-esteem. There was inevitably some overlap between categories. The questionnaire was introduced to the children with an indication of its purpose and two examples on the board. The statements were read out to the children who were asked to respond by marking their level of agreement with each statement on the four-point scale. It took about ten minutes to administer.

The maths assessment and attitude questionnaire were administered to the experimental and comparison groups two weeks before and again one week after the games intervention (inter-test period nine weeks). Children absent for the pre- or post-assessment were assessed in a small separate group the week following the assessment of their class. It was thus possible to compare attainment and attitudes of each group before and after the intervention, and to compare those of the experimental group with those of the comparison group.

Additionally, formative process evaluation was carried out by teacher and researcher: observation, discussion and feedback, video recording, asking the whole experimental group oral evaluation questions and interviewing three pairs of children in detail. The children also kept their own notebooks in which they wrote comments every session about the games and rated them out of 10. At the end of the final games session, five further evaluation questions requiring individual written responses were given to the experimental group. These were also given to the project teacher, together with a more extensive interview and questionnaire.

Process evaluation summary

The attendance of the experimental group was consistently good. For some children in the comparison group it was more erratic, resulting in absence from part of the assessment; two children from the comparison group also left during the term, leaving 20.

Materials

As previously mentioned, there were too many games. The ones which were not played included a number of the laminated Strategy games and some of the older school maths games. Instructions for playing were simplified for most of the games and puzzles provided by the researcher, but a lot of reading was still required. The rules of the games from educational suppliers were generally not simplified, and some of the instructions were confusing and inadequate. The result of this was some initial confusion among some children, with requests for clarification and help.

Observation suggested that the wooden three-dimensional puzzles were very popular, together with 'traditional' games such as Battleship and Mastermind. This was also evident from comments made by children in their notebooks. The games from educational suppliers (e.g. Jungle Climb) looked good but sometimes proved disappointing. The number games – whether from educational suppliers or high street stores – appeared to be less popular than the three-dimensional puzzles and strategy games. The children verbally stated that popular games and puzzles included Mastermind, Connect 4, Switch It, Tower of Hanoi and Arrest (a laminated strategy game). Some children described Battleship and Rhombic Star as 'hard', although the former was the most popular game of all.

The children's later written responses produced slightly different results, with the Puzzles category reported as most popular. Wooden constructional puzzles such as Rhombic Star and Soma Cube seemed to have become particular favourites. The adults also observed that the very simple wooden Lost Marble puzzle produced much enjoyment. Strategy and Shape were the next most popular categories, while Number was hardly mentioned. The most popular game of all was Battleship. Reasons given for the popularity of these games and puzzles were that they were 'challenging' and 'good fun'. Three children suggested that the games 'helped you to read' and one that the games 'helped you with maths'.

The teacher reported that the puzzles and games provided by the researcher had been more successful than the school's games. He felt that the wooden puzzles had been especially worthwhile.

Procedure

The overall impression was that the sessions were successful – the children were absorbed, well-behaved and busy and showed their enthusiasm most of the time. Initially there was some squabbling between pairs but this became less evident over the course of the intervention. Two children who spent the first three sessions accusing each other of cheating settled down and played well for the remainder of the project. One success was the pairing of one of the most able children in the class with one of the least able ones.

The routine procedure was generally followed well. Initially some pairs had difficulty reading and following the games instructions, but considerable improvement occurred over the six-week intervention. Video recording showed the children concentrating very hard on some of the Position and Movement and Strategy games (Battleship, Mastermind, Switch it). There was also evidence of computation: in one or two clips a child was clearly carrying out a written or a mental calculation (e.g. in the game Equality). The Puzzles presented a slightly different picture, but also a positive one. Children were absorbed, concentrating hard, thinking and manipulating. The social aspect was evident but more sporadic, as a child attempted his or her own puzzle then watched another child for a while and maybe asked for help or offered advice.

The notebooks were used as planned and kept well by the children. They put the date, the name of the game and the category, with a comment about whether they had enjoyed playing the game and whether they would recommend it to others. There was a tendency to rate many games 10/10; while 5/10 was a bad rating, signifying 'very boring'. Some children wrote more extended comments which gave a clearer picture of what they thought. Writing comments at the end of each session soon became an established routine, with even poor writers managing to write something.

The video revealed that playing the games was a very social activity, with lots of chatter about the games. There were some arguments initially. Children were keen to win the games and sometimes accused their partners of `cheating'. In the first session there were tears when a boy wanted to use a game which another pair had taken. As the sessions proceeded communication between children appeared to improve. The video strikingly captured the eye contact between pairs working together and their facial expressions and smiling. The children's non-verbal communication showed clearly that the games and puzzles were fun. The cooperative nature of the project in general, and working in pairs in particular, led to informal discussion in the sessions about which games or puzzles the group were playing, discussion of the instructions for play by each pair and much incidental discussion during play. A small amount of whole-class discussion with the class teacher and the researcher took place at the end of the sessions, but this was practical rather than mathematical: thus opportunities for mathematical discussion and questioning were missed.

Cooperation

Video revealed good cooperation in setting out the games, playing them, scoring and putting them away. Minor problems in the early games sessions included group monitors exceeding their remit and not allowing pairs to choose their games, and children asking for help without having read the instructions. There was also one girl whose initial attitude towards the games seemed very negative. Her notebook provided evidence for this – but also presented striking evidence of her conversion after three sessions and her subsequent positive thoughts on the games and puzzles. Her post-test results on the attitude survey also suggested an increase in overall positivity, and a substantial gain was evident in her maths post-test score. The video also revealed one boy sitting disconsolately after his partner had wandered off following a disagreement. Later in the session this pair became absorbed in playing Mastermind, and from this point on the class teacher reported better cooperative working for them. The reduction in squabbling and the increased ability to work both in groups and pairs over the course of the project suggested that progress was made in working cooperatively. Observations of sessions, the class teacher's report and video all supported this.

Outcome evaluation results

Non-parametric statistical tests were carried out on the data.

Attitudes

The overall attitude positivity scores of the experimental and comparison groups were very similar at pre-test and at post-test. This was also true for the attitude sub-tests concerning attitudes to mathematics and to working cooperatively. However, the experimental group did have significantly higher self-esteem scores post-test than pre-test (Wilcoxon Test 2-tailed P = 0.0168). The self-esteem scores for the comparison group were slightly lower at post-test. No significant gender differences were found.

Mathematics Test

There were 30 items in the maths test and the highest possible score was 30. The raw scores of both the experimental group and the comparison group increased from pre-test to post-test. The difference was significant for the experimental group (mean gain = 1.56, Wilcoxon Test: 2-tailed P = 0.0071), but not for the comparison group (mean gain = 0.25).

At pre-test the mean scores of the comparison group were significantly higher than those for the experimental group (Mann-Whitney Test: 2-tailed P = 0.0254). At post-test the difference between comparison and experimental mean scores had narrowed and was no longer statistically significant.

The boys in both groups improved significantly from pre-test to post-test (Wilcoxon Test: 2-tailed P = 0.0178). However, the comparison group girls' performance was slightly worse at post-test than at pre-test, while the experimental group girls' performance was only slightly better at post-test than at pre-test. The gender discrepancy was particularly evident in the experimental group where the improvement of the girls was small and not significant, while the boys' improvement was statistically significant (Wilcoxon Test: 2-tailed P = 0.0281).

Participant evaluation

Children's responses included 'games helped you to share', . . . 'showed why you should read the instructions', and . . . 'helped with maths words and spelling'. Disliked aspects included difficult words and instructions, small print, common games they had played before, boring games, games where people cheat. Improvements could include bigger groups of children to play the games, easier instructions and making some of the puzzles harder.

The teacher felt the project had definitely been worthwhile, reporting that the experimental class (including himself) had learned 'a lot about themselves, meeting challenges, and working together'. The experimental group children were described as becoming more sociable and tolerant and more willing to follow rules and instructions.

The pairing and grouping led the class teacher to consider other different seating arrangements in other curriculum areas.

Discussion

Duration of the intervention

The six-week intervention was arguably too short and the frequency of the sessions too few at two per week. Results might have been better with an eight-week intervention and three games sessions weekly. Little measurable improvement was likely given a total time on task of 10 to 12 hours. Additional optional games access during break times might be considered.

Games

According to participant evaluation, the 'best' games were long-standing traditional games such as Mastermind, Battleship, Connect 4, Uno, Yahtzee, all of which were purchased from stores rather than educational suppliers. The 'best' puzzles were the wooden ones (e.g. Rhombic Star, Soma Cube) which were well-made, aesthetically attractive and challenging.

Rules

Although many rules were simplified, the majority still required a substantial amount of reading. The advantage of this was that children improved in the skill of reading and following the instructions over the course of the intervention. The disadvantage was that weaker readers sometimes struggled.

Groups and the rotation of the games

The rotation of games round the groups and the replacement of games during the project could have been managed better and was not helped by storage problems. The class teacher suggested that a pre-set diagrammatic plan for the rotation of games round the groups would have been helpful.

Monitors

The use of monitors was intended to reduce unnecessary movement in the classroom and increase the children's accountability in looking after the games. Pairs of children in each group took turns to be monitors so that everyone in the group was a monitor for a week. In the early sessions some monitors decided to distribute particular games to pairs in their group rather than letting the pairs make their own choice from the group games. This problem was soon resolved. The children were sensible and careful in their handling of the games and responsible about putting them away. Only one puzzle was broken and all vital pieces of games and puzzles were present and intact at the end of the project. The system seemed to have worked well, although much of this may have been due to the class teacher's good organisation and relationship with his class. It cannot be assumed that projects in all classes would proceed as smoothly.

Discussing mathematics

'Mathematical' discussion and questioning between teacher and children has been recommended by a number of writers (Skemp 1989a, Whitebread 1995, Askew and Wiliam 1995). Although communication improved and chatter and body language indicated much enjoyable communication related to the games, more appropriate questioning by the teacher and the researcher during the sessions might have encouraged the development of higher-quality mathematical thinking and problem-solving strategies in the children.

Validity and reliability of attitude measure

The attitude questionnaire was not piloted and there was no information as to its reliability or validity. However, test–retest scores were so nearly identical for both groups as to suggest a high degree of test–retest reliability. The children's post-project attitudes to mathematics may have remained unchanged in reality. They had enjoyed the games and puzzles, but knew that there would be no more games sessions. Why should this have made them more positive towards mathematics in general? Observation indicated a more positive attitude to working cooperatively, in contrast to the questionnaire findings. However, whether this would continue post-project is unclear and would depend on a number of factors, not least the provision of further opportunities for cooperative working.

Validity and reliability of mathematics assessment

The mathematics test aimed at clarity and simplicity, focusing on mathematical vocabulary and some tasks and situations of the kind that would be met in the mathematical games. At post-test it may have favoured the experimental group who had played the games. However, the brevity of the intervention must be taken into account, and also that a number of the questions related to situations and mathematical vocabulary in the laminated strategy games which were hardly used at all. Some regression to the mean was evident in the post-test scores of the comparison group, particularly the boys, although not in the experimental group. It was also possible that there was a degree of ceiling effect in the results, particularly for high-scoring girls in the comparison group, although the mean post-test score was only 20 out of 30.

Gender differences

The mathematics test indicated gains for boys but not for girls. While there might be artefactual elements in this finding, it appears that the Paired Maths approach did not positively discriminate in favour of girls. However, this might be influenced by same-gender pairings, as Topping and Whiteley (1993) found with Paired Reading.

Hawthorne Effect

A further possibility was that any improvements in the experimental group may have resulted from the Hawthorne Effect – the impact of extra attention and novelty alone. This is true of many classroom interventions. Ideally, additional follow-up evaluation should be carried out three months later.

Action implications

Further research should utilise measures of known reliability and validity or establish the reliability and validity of newly-created measures. The use of comparison groups which are totally comparable and the gathering of follow-up data are highly desirable. How long it is realistic to expect the effect of a relatively slight intervention to endure is a difficult issue, however. Further examination of differential gender effects in relation to variation in organisational parameters is necessary. In addition to cross-gender matching, the use of extrinsic rewards, subjects of a different age, cross-age pairing, and interventions of different duration and frequency could all be explored. If these were evaluated rigorously it should be possible to draw conclusions about the most cost-effective intervention. Comparison of the Paired Maths approach with more traditional cooperative learning, using structured activities more closely coupled with the formal curriculum, would also be of interest.

There are implications here for making more effective use of mathematical games in the classroom, and for including a wider variety of mathematical puzzles and games, purchased from stores, stemming from ancient times or traditionally in the public domain. There are implications, too, that schools should monitor and assess the relative progress of girls and boys in the learning of mathematics in relation to teaching methods in use, and that teachers might usefully monitor their own interactions with girls and boys in the classroom.

CHAPTER 7

Cross-school peer tutoring in maths for special needs

This chapter describes a collaborative project designed to promote integration, operated between one class in a special school for severe learning difficulty children and many children in a mainstream primary school, alternately in each location. The project involved structured cross-school cross-ability reciprocal peer tutoring in Makaton and mathematics, using a variety of carefully selected 'real life' games for the latter. Evaluation in cognitive, social and affective domains was by naturalistic observation. The viability of the approach with children with severe learning difficulties is discussed, as are the gains accruing to pupils from both establishments.

The reflective practitioner will draw much from this report which could also be applied to cross-ability peer-tutored Paired Science projects involving pupils with special educational needs, in addition to the guidance on organisation already provided in Chapter three of this book.

Background

Social integration initiatives for children with severe learning difficulties developed apace and showed great promise through the 1980s. For instance, many special schools made arrangements to 'twin' with local mainstream schools, in the hope that shared experiences would offer a wider range of stimulation and modelling to the exceptional children and broaden the awareness of the mainstream children.

However, it was not always easy to structure these shared experiences so that they were mutually productive – merely 'being there' was hardly true integration. As the financial climate in education worsened and teachers in mainstream and special schools struggled to cope with the National Curriculum and the torrent of other changes, such initiatives were increasingly in danger of abandonment as low priority.

Fortunately teachers are remarkably resilient. Worthwhile enterprises continued to develop and attitudes on all sides became still more open (Carpenter *et al.* 1991). Meanwhile special schools themselves undertook a drive towards curricular 'normalisation', as they strove to relate the National Curriculum framework to the special needs of their pupils.

In the mathematics area, this latter movement resulted in a number of useful publications, such as those from East Sussex County Council (1990), Robbins (1991), Manchester Teacher Fellows (1993) and Sebba *et al.* (1993). In this context, interest grew in the use of mathematical games, since children with learning difficulties seemed above all others to need to learn mathematical concepts in an interactive, experiential way. The work of Roy McConkey and Dorothy Jeffree has been seminal in this field (see McConkey and McEvoy 1986, McConkey 1987; Jeffree 1989).

Partially as a reflection of the increasing demands to 'do more with less', interest in peer tutoring as a structured vehicle for promoting interactive and cooperative learning has also surged in recent years (Topping 1988, Topping and Ehly 1998). Research evidence has accumulated on the effective involvement of special needs pupils as both tutees and tutors (Osguthorpe and Scruggs 1990, Scruggs and Mastropieri 1997), the latter serving to underscore the valuing of the individual and his or her unique strengths. Reciprocal peer tutoring has become increasingly common in groups of 'normal' ability (Topping 1992), but is as yet rare with mixed special needs and mainstream groups.

Context and organisation

In Highfields special school for children with severe learning difficulties, almost all classes are 'linked' with a different local mainstream school. In Class 7 there are eight children aged 12 to 14 who participate in weekly exchange visits with St Patrick's Primary School. One week the Highfields children visit St Patrick's and the next week the other way around.

A visit *to* Highfields typically consists of between 8 and 10 Year 6 primary school children from one of two such parallel classes visiting Class 7 for an afternoon. The following week four members of Class 7 go *from* Highfields to St Patrick's for an afternoon.

The link facilitates social integration on both sides. Fortunately the schools are within walking distance. Teachers from the two schools always meet in September to plan and update the programme for the year. The Class 7 teacher also gives a talk to Year 6 parents in St Patrick's, explaining the programme to them early in the new academic year. The parents have always been very approving of the link.

Outline of activities

The primary school pupils are prepared for a visit to Highfields by their own class teacher, through explanation and discussion. Activities are organised and guided by the Class 7 teacher. There are a variety of introduction games (including a musical one) and news is exchanged. The Highfields pupils teach the St Patrick's pupils some Makaton signs to help them communicate while in the special school and practice of Makaton signing usually follows.

After a session in the ball pool and refreshments prepared by the 'hosts' the visitors are much more settled and confident and have begun expressing their curiosity about life in Highfields. The primary pupils assist Class 7 pupils with dressing and choose their partners for playing games.

The following week the Highfields teacher takes four pupils to St Patrick's. They are met in the playground by the host pupils who had visited Highfields the previous week. Afternoon school begins with music in the hall. The Highfields pupils have little difficulty conforming to the organisation and rules of the session. Irrespective of disability, the children then climb two flights of stairs for an interchange of news and free discussion with a whole class. The primary school children feel free to ask further questions and some wish to refresh the Makaton being learnt.

The Highfields children then leave the whole class and adjourn to the library with the host pupils. In addition to mathematical games, pairs use computers and share story books. The host children prepare refreshments at playtime and then everyone goes out into a playground containing over 200 children. After break, activities continue as before. The following week a different set of primary school pupils renew the cycle.

Mutual benefits

During these interactions the Highfields pupils are learning to mix with larger and much more varied groups of peers and adults, cope with different physical environments and make decisions regarding choice of partner, activity and game. They are also exposed to a much wider range of behavioural expectations.

During the peer tutoring activities, the Highfields children benefit from a 2 : 1 tutorial ratio – considerably better than most schools can offer! As the linking arrangements are reciprocal, even members of the Highfields class who are not able to cope with a visit to a primary school are able to receive visits from mainstream pupils in the familiar and secure context of their own classroom. The two-way linkage also means that the eight primary school pupils who in turn welcome the Highfields pupils to their school develop bonds which are sustained for longer than one brief meeting. As well as developing caring and hospitable attitudes, the primary pupils come to know the limitations and needs of individual Highfields children in some detail.

The primary school teachers feel it is important that their pupils' personal and social education includes contact with those who are perhaps less able intellectually but who nevertheless have other valuable skills and personal characteristics to offer. The primary school pupils have learnt Makaton signs very quickly and enjoy using these with their own families as well as with Highfields pupils. The mainstream pupils enjoy the experience of helping, but generally avoid an excess of sentiment or pity and can be quite hard taskmasters. Many of the primary school pupils do subsequent topic work or projects on various aspects of disability. There is a mutual exchange of greetings cards at Christmas and Easter. The primary school perform a pantomime in Highfields to enable all Highfields pupils to enjoy it. These positive relationships extend into chance meetings out in the local community.

Mathematical games

The mathematical games used in this peer tutoring context were selected:

- to be enjoyable,
- to allow equal competition between the pair,
- to be easy to understand,
- to encourage discussion and the development of mathematical language,
- to be flexible and allow extension activities,
- to be attractive and well packaged,
- to be inexpensive and,
- to not look like 'schoolwork' (see Chapter 2).

They were mostly three-dimensional, a mix of items carefully selected from toyshops and those produced from everyday materials on a 'cottage industry' basis. All posed mathematical problems and required mathematical skills in their solution, generalised into what was for many children a novel situation, but nevertheless linked to National Curriculum requirements. The games were grouped into categories according to the predominant mathematical content featured within them: Matching/Bonds, Shape, Ordering, Pattern/ Strategies, Conservation and Counting.

Given the Highfields pupils' special needs, games at the developmental level of average 5 to 7-year-olds (Key Stage 1) seemed the most appropriate basis for peer tutoring usage in the context of the mainstream link scheme. A small kit of games especially for this project was created by selecting a cross-section of the games in a standard kit at this level. Criteria for choice included:

- durability,
- safety,
- brevity,
- manipulability,
- attractiveness,
- low distraction,
- compactness and cohesion of pieces,
- size,
- quality of instructions,
- goal orientation,
- age appropriateness,
- multi-sensory aspects and,
- variety of levels of complexity.

Subsequently the whole of the mainstream primary class were allowed to familiarise themselves with the rules and materials of a variety of games and decide which they liked best and which were most feasible for the Highfields children. The most popular and practically usable games are listed by category below:

1. *Conservation:* Dogimoes, Connect 4.
2. *Matching/bonds:* Snap (various), Huff Puff.
3. *Counting:* Scaredy Cat, Incy Wincy Spider, Snakes and Ladders.
4. *Ordering:* Dragon Game, Climb the Beanstalk, The Old Woman who Lived in a Shoe.
5. *Pattern/relation:* Ladybirds.
6. *Shape:* Pass the Bag, Attribute Bingo.

The mathematical games were played every week in both schools for 20 to 30 minutes. A game would be played by two, three or four pupils depending upon the choice of the pupils themselves and the format of the game.

Interactive behaviour

The primary school children were very fair but firm. They encouraged the Highfields pupils but expected them to participate fully in throwing a dice, counting and generally keeping to the rules. They proved very adept at explaining and simplifying the rules where necessary. During the sessions a great deal of language usage was evident, mathematical vocabulary being introduced, explained and reinforced by the primary school pupils. Words such as 'more', 'less', and so forth began to appear more frequently in the vocabulary of the Highfields pupils. All of the pupils laughed a great deal, and the Highfields pupils thoroughly enjoyed the one-to-one attention and the element of competition, since of course the aspect of random chance in many games meant anyone could win or lose.

During these sessions, many of the Highfields pupils showed entirely different facets of their personality. Some hitherto rather passive pupils became much more enlivened, extrovert and interested. Pupils usually quiet became considerably more verbal. Others proved surprisingly quick to learn. A socially withdrawn child became more responsive to other children.

The primary school pupils also benefited and often it was the less able primary school child who shone in this situation. Some were initially very shy, but all were interested and very willing. Teachers from both schools came to see their pupils in a different light and there was the additional merit of feeling that special school pupils and staff were kept in contact not only with mainstream children but also with mainstream teachers.

As the weeks went by the Highfields pupils learnt increasingly sophisticated skills, both specific and general. Thus improvements in specific skills of matching and ordering were paralleled with development in general skills such as turn-taking. Preferences for individual games become more clearly defined. Incy Wincy Spider, Pass the Bag, Climb the Beanstalk, Connect 4, Ladybirds, and Snap Games proved the most popular. In some games the playing pieces were still too small to hold and too difficult to manipulate. The variety of games available meant that boredom did not set in, pupils being quick to discard the less popular games.

Implications

From direct naturalistic teacher observation, gains seemed to accrue in the cognitive, social and affective domains. However, it would be difficult indeed to evaluate in quantitative terms the full range of outcomes for either set of pupil participants. Many variables were in operation and the ascription of particular gains to specific causative factors with any validity would prove problematic. Attempts to separate out the impact of individual factors by quasi-experiments would risk destroying the organic effectiveness of the whole.

The value of the total scheme in terms of social interaction, language development, skill learning and sheer enjoyment was however very obvious to the teachers during the sessions. The scheme made accessible for Highfields pupils many games which were previously considered beyond their competence. Some gains were observed to generalise across time and space. Some Highfields pupils can now play some of the games with a minimum of supervision with a fellow Highfields classmate.

Highfields pupils learned a great deal of mathematical language and along the way acquired a certain amount of reading sight vocabulary – for instance discrimination between 'yes' and 'no' on a dice, 'start' and 'finish' on a board and so on. Levels of concentration on games increased considerably. Perhaps the most telling evaluative indicator was the frequent requests to the class teacher to play mathematical games at other times.

Certainly well-organised reciprocal peer tutoring can be recommended as a positive framework for truly integrationist experiences. Given wider use of this methodology, more quantitative evaluation research should become possible.

Acknowledgements

With thanks to the following: Kathy Bradley and Chris Sutcliffe from St Patrick's Roman Catholic Junior and Infants School, David Howson, John Shipman and other participating staff from Highfields School.

CHAPTER 8

Conclusions and future directions

This chapter briefly summarises the state of the art in the development of Paired Maths and Paired Science, and discusses possible future developments and research, including the impact of information technology and increasing access to cooperative mathematical and scientific activities in the home via the Internet independent of schools.

Paired Maths and Science: the state of the art

The main thrust of this book (and its two companion volumes) is based on the assertion that mathematics and science matter. Their importance should however be conceived and addressed more broadly than has previously been done by many schools.

Mathematics and science are important for the individual and for the nation, and at all levels in-between. Maths and science are important economically, cognitively, affectively and socially. Maths and science are more important outwith school than inside it.

Given wider acceptance of 'lifelong learning' as an urgent need, as a new reality, and as an entitlement, education systems in general and schools in particular need to reconceptualise their role, not least as developments in information technology move us daily nearer the 'virtual school'.

Paired Maths and Paired Science are systems for parents, peers and other non-professional tutors to interact with children using specifically selected and structured mathematical games and scientific activities which are unlike ordinary schoolwork. The aim is to consolidate and deepen understanding and to generalise problem-solving skills out of the classroom into 'real-life' community settings, as well as increasing enjoyment, motivation and confidence in all partners.

Key distinguishing features of Paired Maths and Paired Science include emphasis upon:

- positive attitudes, feelings, confidence, self-belief,
- generalisation of skills to life outside school,
- language and discussion to test and extend understanding,

- supportive structure and personal choice combined,
- self-sustaining gains and satisfaction for all participants,
- durable, robust and widely replicable methods,
- access and equal opportunities for all.

Paired Maths and Paired Science have been better researched than many innovations in education, a field which has been all too prone to large expensive mistakes driven by current ideology, value judgements or politics.

In Paired Maths, there is hard evidence of cognitive impact for Level 1 parental involvement and Level 2 same-age peer tutoring (although not yet cross-age peer tutoring or Level 3). Positive structured subjective feedback has come from a number of schools, including at Level 3. Successful extension to children with severe learning difficulties and English as a second language has been reported. In Paired Science, only Level 1 activities have been available so far, and positive structured subjective feedback has been reported from three schools.

Future research

In both Paired Maths and Paired Science, further research could encompass both cognitive and affective outcomes for Levels 1, 2 and 3, for parental involvement, same-age peer tutoring and cross-age peer tutoring. Such research should seek to include comparison or control groups, utilise multiple instrumentation, and extend to medium- or long-term follow-up evaluation. High levels of participant enthusiasm are not the same as measurable cognitive outcomes, and the one should not lead to presupposition of the other. Given the objectives and nature of Paired Maths and Paired Science, evaluation should be of:

- affective as well as cognitive outcomes,
- skill as well as knowledge,
- verbal discourse as well as written outcomes,
- 'real life' as well as 'school' applications, and
- all participants, not just the tutee children.

Particularly with mathematics, changes in participant perceptions of the face validity of the games and activities (i.e. changes in their definition of what is mathematics) would also be an impact indicator of interest.

Merely because Paired Maths and Paired Science *can* be effective, it does not follow that they must automatically always be so everywhere. Clear and detailed descriptions of, and process data on, operation of the methods must be provided in subsequent research, so that implementation integrity can be determined by external readers and to enable accurate replication of successful projects. Where projects have deployed multiple intervention strategies, some means for partialling out the specific effects of each is needed. Wide replication of these methods should further illuminate their durability and robustness, and their application on an equal opportunity basis to all potential contexts and consumers (including exploration of any gender differential impact).

Experimentation with the methods applied to a variety of more challenging populations could prove illuminating in relation to use with 'ordinary' children also.

Let us now turn to likely future developments in mathematics and science learning which have implications for subsequent adaptations of Paired Maths and Paired Science as described in this book and its companion volumes.

Computer-supported collaborative work in maths and science

A great deal of computer software to develop mathematical and scientific abilities is now available. Much of this is suitable for use at home as well as school. However, early software was, and some still is, very primitive, offering little more than worksheets on screen. The addition of multimedia or hypermedia elements to such programmes do little to enhance their utility, merely providing distraction. So schools and parents (and children) need to choose software carefully – seeking intelligent and adaptive programmes which require interactivity by the child and which offer the child feedback and prompts to develop meta-cognitive skills.

However, computer-delivered instruction should not serve as a substitute for human interaction. Human support, feedback and (above all) discussion remain essential, and can focus on computer-delivered material and games just as easily as on lines scratched in the sand and pebbles. Computer supported collaborative work between pairs at home or in the classroom is likely to increasingly offer alternative games and activities in both mathematics and science, but the software will only be as intelligent as the person who wrote it.

Maths and science at home through the Internet

Interactive maths and science programmes are now also increasingly available at a distance, through the World Wide Web. Again it is important that these are a focus for human interaction, not a substitute for it.

Examples in mathematics (also see Appendix 5)

The US Department of Education (Office of Educational Research and Improvement) has a site with details of many maths games for parents to play with their children, as well as more general information for parents.
(http://www.ed.gov/pubs/parents/Math/index.html)

'Mathematics for Parents' is a series of electronic newsletters for parents interested in helping their children with mathematics. It aims to help parents understand how their children think mathematically, and covers:

- number,
- mathematics and writing,
- shape and space,

- nets,
- multiplication,
- measurement of length and area,
- place value,
- division, and
- spatial reasoning.

(http://www.wcer/wisc.edu/Projects/Mathematics for Parents
email jhorvath@macc.wisc.edu)

'Math Resources' is a website which indexes a number of other sites, including:

- a gallery of interactive geometry,
- math magic,
- geometry newsgroups (if you can't figure out the answer, someone else in the world probably can!),
- Mega-Math,
- Fun Math,
- Ask Dr Math, and so on.

(http://www.teleport.com/~vincer/math.html)

More able pairs (children and parents!) can discuss the meaning of infinity through the online MathClub.

Examples in science

Parents and children will increasingly be able to download from the Internet guidelines for scientific investigations at home and out in the community. There are already some such World Wide Web sites (and many more on science activities in the classroom which could perhaps be adapted), but many change too frequently to be worth listing here. However, the ERIC Clearinghouse for Science, Mathematics and Environmental Education (http://www.ericse.org) and the US Government Department of Education (http://www.ed.gov) are good places to start.

Regular Internet searches using the key words 'parents' (or 'family' or 'home') and 'science' will yield more each time they are done. Children are already discussing science by email, and computer-based collaborative scientific problem-solving at a distance is becoming common. However, the social and emotional impact of participating in a group project in partnership with your neighbourhood school and other parents and children in your own community is unlikely ever to be satisfactorily replicated by a computer.

Ever onwards and upwards

For the future, a repertoire of approaches of known effectiveness to suit different purposes and contexts in the ecology of the host community should be developed. Hopefully you, the reader, will play a significant part in these developments. The authors and contributors to this book and its two companion volumes wish you good luck in your endeavours.

Details of Paired Maths project games: Levels 1, 2 and 3

1a Further details of selected items in the Key Stage 1 games kit

Counting

1 Snakes and Ladders (also see Ludo)
A chance game involving counting backwards and forwards and anticipation. Age range: 4 to 12. Available from most toyshops.

2 Insey Winsey Spider
Four boards with four spiders, a spinner and a dice. The object is to get the spider into his (her?) web at the top of the drainpipe. Age range: 3 to 8. Available from NES Arnold (see Appendix 2). Can be split into two separate games.

3 Scaredy Cat
Set of cards with blackbirds and pieces of scarecrow to complete. Involves counting and matching. Age range: 4 to 8. Available from NES Arnold.

Conservation

1 Button Box
Collection of different buttons with instructions on different ways of sorting them. Age range: 3 to 5. Available from Grandma's button box. Make sure there is enough variety for the suggested activities.
   Suggested Activity Card:

   (i)   Can you sort for the same: SHAPE, or SIZE, or COLOUR or NUMBER? Which are exactly the same?
   (ii) Make a row of different buttons – take turns to try to copy it.
   (iii) Put out four different buttons. Cover and take one away – which one is missing?
   (iv) Put all the buttons in a row, starting with the biggest, ending with the smallest.

2 Connect 4
Plastic board which stands up and has rows and columns of slots to take counters of two different colours. Age range: 4 to 14. Available from good toyshops. Can also be included in Patterns.
   Suggested Activity Card:

   (i)   Sort out the colours. How many are there?
   (ii) Make the wall half red and half yellow. How many ways can you do this?
   (iii) How many patterns can you make?
   (iv) Roll a dice, take turns to put in the counters (a) who is highest? (b) how many more to be equal?
   (v)   Try to get four in a line. Can you stop each other?

Pattern/Relation

1 Pick A Button
Set of buttons which match according to different properties.
Object: to match the buttons according to the rules and to get rid of all the buttons. Age range: 3
to 8. Can be assembled at home. Spinner can be made out of cardboard and pencil.
   Suggested Activity Card: Rules

(i)   Each player takes it in turn to choose a button from the box until each has six buttons,
(ii) The king button is placed on the table,
(iii) Players take it in turns to spin the spinner and must match the last button put on the table
      with the property displayed on the spinner,
(iv) The first to get rid of all their buttons is the winner.

2 Mosaics
Box with different plastic shapes and a sample pattern. Object: to make up pattern in turns. The
loser places the last piece. Age range: 3 to 8. Can be assembled at home from any box of different
plastic shapes.
   Suggested Activity Card:

(i)   Can you sort the pieces for same shapes and same colours?
(ii) Can you fit some of the small pieces on top of the bigger ones?
(iii) Can you make a pattern? Take turns to copy each other.
(iv) Can you make a picture?
(v)   How many pieces can you fit together without spaces?

Ordering

1 Cards – Rummy
Pack of playing cards with instructions. Winner has to get three or more cards of the same suit in
the correct order. Age range: 5 to 15. Cards available from most toyshops; instructions simplified
from a playing-card game book (e.g. Collins Gem Card Games, Harper Collins, Glasgow, 1991).

2 Hundred Square Jigsaw
Base board with numbers 1 to 100 and jigsaw pieces to fit it. The loser is the one who places the
last piece on the board. Age range: 6 to 8. Available from NORMAC (see Appendix 2).
   Suggested Activity Card: Use this as an ordinary jigsaw or play the following game:

(i)   Share the pieces equally between you,
(ii) Decide who will start,
(iii) The first player places a piece on the board. The second player places another piece on the
      board – but only if it adjoins a yellow square,
(iv) Take turns until all the pieces are on the board.

   The loser is the one who places the last piece on the board.

Matching/Bonds

1 Humpty Dumpty
Cards of different figures with matching base. Objective: to complete the Humpty Dumpty and
gain the most men. Involves counting and matching. Age range: 3 to 6. Available from NES
Arnold. Can be split in two sets.

2 Beetle
Four sets of head, body, limbs, etc., plus one dice. Object: to assemble your beetle first. Age range: 3 to 8. Available from good toyshops. Can be split up into two games by adding another dice.

3 Snap and Number Snap
Eighteen pairs of cards with numbers. Object: to win all the cards. Age range: 3 to 14. Available from good toyshops.
   Suggested Activity Card:

(i)   Match the same pictures.
(ii) Put a line of different pictures to copy.
(iii) Put out four pairs face down – take turns to turn up one and find the pairs.
(iv) Play SNAP.
(v)   How many cards are the same?
(vi) How many pairs are there?

Shape

1 Pass The Bag
Four boards, four bags, 40 pieces to match pictures on boards. Players take turns to pick a shape from the bag without seeing it. Age range: 4 to 9. Bag and board can be home-made, used with any purchased or made set of shapes. Can be split into two, if one new bag is added.
   Suggested Activity Card:

(i)   Sorting – sort the pieces for shape, size, colour.
(ii) Lotto – caller takes out one piece at a time – first full card wins.
(iii) Pass the bag – take it in turns to take a shape from the bag without looking – wrong colours are put back – the first full card wins.

2 Mr Space Game
Different shapes to fit a figure on a board. Dice are used to enable player to place shape on board. Winner is the one who completes figure first. Age range: 4 to 8. Available from NES Arnold. Can be split to make two games.

1b Key Stage 2 games

Strategy – yellow	*Spatial – red*	*Number – green*
Tip It	Continuo	Little Professor
Guess Who	Crazy Connections	Frog Jump
Mastermind	Leap Frog	Shut The Box
Number Game	Car Capers	Ono 99
Battleships	Mr Space	Teachers' Pet
Peg Game	Triangulo	Bingo
Pik-a-Styx	Take a Train	Uno
		Tiddley Winks
		Greed

Relations – orange

Goldilocks
Coppit
Frustration
Finders Keepers
Crossing Game
Rods
Whot
White Rabbit

Puzzles – blue

Colourtair
Squaring the Circle
Peg Solitaire
Tangrams
Playcube
Hundred Square Jigsaw
Outwit
Crazy Witch
Crazy Turtle
Crazy Plane

1c Key Stage 3 games

In each category, three-dimensional games are above the dotted line, supplementary two-dimensional games below it.

Puzzles (blue)

Number	Puzzle	Number	Puzzle
1	Disappearing Square	7	Rubik's Cube
2	Squaring the Circle	8	Rubik's Clock
3	Perfect Squares	9	Thinkominos
4	Serpent	10	Tangrams
5	Polydron Playcube	11	Triangle Game
6	Rubik's Magic	12	Frogs
13	Square Puzzles	35	Rabbit Relations
14	Counterfeat 1	36	Endless Lines
15	Counterfeat 2	37	What's the Difference?
16	Counterfeat 3	38	Number Crozzle
17	Counterpath	39	Stick At It
18	Diviso	40	Mystery Tour
19	Counterpart	41	Treasure Map
20	Dump	42	Solitaire
21	Antisocial Puzzle	43	Marvellous 26
22	Counterswitch	44	Hex Hop
23	Number Path	45	Card Solitaires
24	Counterline	46	Addition Puzzle
25	Monster's Wardrobe	47	Pentalpha
26	Shopping on Mars	48	Penny Solitaire
27	United Shirts	49	Treble Interchange
28	Calculation	50	Vanishing Squares
29	Baking on Mars	51	Magic Triangles
30	Self-destruct	52	Packing
31	Block Saw	53	Birthdays
32	Squares	54	Number Squares
33	Martian Maths	55	Number Crossword
34	Hieroglyphics	56	Mathword

57	Countermore	63	The Design
58	Code Wheelies	64	Distort
59	Darts	65	Sequences
60	Number Quest	66	Word Symmetry
61	Relations	67	Word Search
62	Stripping	68	Haunted House

Strategy (yellow)

Number	Game	Number	Game
1	Clash	8	Tactics
2	Uno	9	Space Orbiter/ Pong Hau K'i
3	5 in a Row	10	Grasshopper
4	Othello	11	Entangle
5	Labyrinth	12	Encircle
6	Tic Tac Toe	13	Enforce
7	Star Base	14	Enfold
15	Noro	32	Serpents
16	Achi	33	Mu Torere
17	Catch Me	34	Royal Game of Ur
18	3 Men's Morris	35	Palm Tree
19	6 Men's Morris	36	Ludus Latrunculorum
20	9 Men's Morris	37	High Jump
21	12 Men's Morris	38	Kono
22	Poker	39	Fighting Serpents
23	Seega	40	Yote
24	Matchin Min	41	Konane
25	Trios	42	Go
26	Mosaic	43	Asalto
27	Crocogator	44	Nyout
28	Necklace	45	Zohn Ahl
29	Stack of Chips	46	Patolli
30	Trap the Pig	47	Puluc
31	Move Move	48	Tablan

Space (red)

Number	Game	Number	Game
1	Devil's Triangle	8	Change Over
2	Triominos	9	Enthrall
3	Shuttles	10	Engage
4	Action Replay	11	Ensnare
5	Nine Rabbit Warren	12	Engender
6	Fighting Snakes	13	Entomb
7	Springboard		
14	Shapes in a Row 4 x 4	26	Navigrid
15	Shapes in a Row 5 x 5	27	Avoid
16	King Monster	28	Cox's Boxes

17	Lau Kati Kata		29	Dead End
18	Fox and Geese		30	Tri-Stix
19	Tablut		31	Quadrangle
20	Alquerque		32	Starslide
21	Star Game		33	Tri-Box
22	Dara		34	Square Box
23	Sz' Kwa		35	Hex Box
24	Knotty Problems		36	Triads
25	Treasure		37	Pathway

Number (green)

(Games 12–22 are card games)

Number	Game		Number	Game
1	Equality		13	Cheat
2	Checkmath		14	Sweet 16
3	Rummikub		15	Go!
4	Little Professor		16	Blackjack
5	Yahtzee		17	500 Rummy
7	Pass the Pigs		18	Product Grid
8	Woof Woof		19	What's My Rule?
9	Gruesome Games		20	Multiples Rummy
10	Number Race		21	Twenty-Nine
11	Pirate Ludo		22	Tough Beans
12	Soccer			

- -

Number	Game		Number	Game
23	Square 15 (3 x 3)		36	Combinations
24	Fifteen (5 x 5)		37	Curly Combinations
25	Sea Battle		38	Sidewinder
26	Digital Noughts & Crosses		39	Bandits
27	Guess My Number		40	Make Ten
28	Calculator Snooker		41	Pirate Fight
29	Circle Nim		42	Tell Us Something New
30	Rectangular Numbers		43	Calculator Tricks
31	Taylor's Game		44	Line of Four
32	Number Grids		45	Catch
33	Nim/Marienbad		46	Grand National
34	Odds On		47	Tables Snap
35	Greed		48	Multichance

Extension (orange)

P = Puzzle G = Game

Number	Game/puzzle		Number	Game/puzzle
1 G	Rubik's Illusion		6 P	Rubik's Triamid
2 G	Rage		7 P	Rubik's Dice
3 G	Pit		8 P	Rubik's Fifteen
4 G	Sting		9 P	Rubik's Tangle
5 P	The 36 Square			

- -

10	P	Tower of Brahma	15	P	Prisoner's Nightmare
11	P	Magic Squares	16	G	Tabula
12	P	Spirals	17	G	Casino
13	P	Knight's Move	18	G	Rithmomachia
14	G	Congclak (Mancala)			

APPENDIX 2

List of suppliers of games and other useful addresses

The following toyshops, stationers and big stores stock a particularly good selection of board games and puzzles in the run-up to Christmas:

- Beatties,
- Hamleys,
- The London Toy Company,
- John Menzies,
- John Lewis,
- Toys 'R' Us.

David Singmaster maintains an extensive list of European game and puzzle suppliers, and relevant magazines, societies and museums. Contact Professor D. Singmaster, Computing Information Systems and Mathematics, South Bank University, London SE1 0AA.

Some of the following suppliers will send catalogues on request:

Beaver Books/Arrow Books, 62–65 Chandos Place, London WC2N 4NW.
Big Box Games, Artstraws Ltd, Unit 3 Clarkeway, Winch Wen Industrial Estate, Swansea.
Crown & Andrews UK Ltd, Wellington House, Kentwood Hill, Tilehurst, Reading, Berks.
Early Learning Centre, South Marston Industrial Estate, Swindon, Wiltshire SN3 4TJ.
Edprint, 234 Holyhead Road, Wellington, Telford, Shropshire TF1 2DZ. Tel. 01952 48623.
Falcon Games Ltd, Travellers Lane, North Mymms, Hatfield, Herts.
James Galt & Co Ltd, Brookfield Road, Cheadle, Cheshire SK8 2PN.
Gibson's Games, Greenlea Park, Prince George's Road, London SW19.
Grant Trading, 1 Morland Avenue, Croydon, Surrey CRO 6EA. Tel/fax. 0181 656 8374.
Harbutts Educational Services, Bretton Way, Bretton, Peterborough PE3 8YA.
Hippo Books, Scholastic Publications, 7–9 Pratt Street, London NW1 OAE.
House Martin International Ltd, Castle Gate, Oulton, Leeds LS26 8HG. (Good value, e.g. Chinese Chequers, Three in a Row)
Icarus Co (Toys) Ltd, Unit 1 Roundways Industrial Estate, Elliott Road, Bournemouth, Dorset.
Kenner Parker Toys International, Hargrave House, Belmont Road, Maidenhead, Berks.
Lagoon Games, PO Box 311, Kingston upon Thames, KT2 5QW.
The London Toy Company, Mail Order Division, Warehouse 431B, Alexandra Avenue, Harrow, Middlesex, HA2 9SG. Tel. 0181 864 2186.
The Longfield Press (Alan Parr), 6 Longfield Gardens, Tring, Herts HP23 4DN. Tel. 01442 824173.
Matchbox Toys, Swaines Industrial Estate, Ashingdon Road, Rochford, Essex SS4 1RH. Tel. 01788 547677.
Milton Bradley Ltd, Hasbro-Bradley UK Ltd, 2 Roundwood Avenue, Stockley Park, Uxbridge, Middlesex UB11 1AZ.
NES Arnold Ltd, Ludlow Hill Road, West Bridgford, Nottingham NG2 6HD.

NORMAC Publications, North Manchester Mathematics Centre, Charlestown Junior School, Pilkington Road, Manchester M9 2BH.

Orchard Toys, Debdale Lane, Keyworth, Nottingham NG12 5HN.

Polydron (UK) Ltd, Unit 11, Brackmills Industrial Estate, Scotia Close, Northampton NN4 OHR.

PUZZLES, Wallop, Hampshire. Tel. 01264 781833.

QED Books, 1 Straylands Grove, York Y03 OEB. Can supply many mathematical titles.

Ravensburger Toys, Fisher-Price Ltd, P0 Box 100, Peterlee, County Durham DH8 2RF.

Scholastic Ltd, Westfield Road, Southam, Leamington Spa, Warwickshire CV33 OJH. Tel. 01926 813910, Fax 01926 817727. Photocopiable shape, space, measures and number games.

Shoptaugh Games Inc, Oakland CA 94618, USA.

J. W. Spear & Sons plc, Richard House, Enstone Road, Enfield, Middlesex EN3 7TB

M. Stanfield Ltd, Murdock Road, Bicester, Oxon OX6 7RH. Tel. 01869 324873.

Tarquin Publications, Stradbroke, Diss, Norfolk IP21 5JP. Tel. 01379 984218, Fax 01379 384 289. Excellent selection of games, puzzles and materials, including Dime materials.

Taskmaster Ltd, Morris Road, Leicester LE2 6BR. Tel. 0116 2704286, Fax 0116 2706992. Equipment, dice, counters, etc. and some games, e.g. Space Shot, Rogues Gallery.

Texas Instruments Ltd, Manton Lane, Bedford MK41 7PA.

Waddingtons Games Ltd, Castle Gate, Oulton, Leeds LS26 8HG. Tel. 0113 2826195.

Wellingtons Ltd, Stamford, Lincolnshire. Fiendish puzzles.

APPENDIX 3

List of games and puzzle books

Allison, A. (1995) *Maths From Rhymes*. Birmingham: Questions Publishing Company.

Ball, J. (undated) *Games From Around the World*. Produced by Benn Associates for Smarties.

Barry, B. (1978) *Hip Pocket Maths Games*. Sydney: Harcourt Brace Jovanovich.

Barry, B. (1979) *More Hip Pocket Maths Games*. Sydney: Harcourt Brace Jovanovich. (Specifically for parents and children.)

Bell, R. and Cornelius, M. (1988) *Board Games Around The World: A Resource Book For Mathematical Investigations*. Cambridge: Cambridge University Press (ISBN 0521359244)

Bolt, B. (1984) *The Amazing Mathematical Amusement Arcade*. Cambridge: Cambridge University Press (ISBN 0521269806) (also see *The Mathematical Funfair* by B. Bolt).

Bolt, B. (1996) *A Mathematical Jamboree*. Cambridge: Cambridge University Press.

Brighouse, A., Godber, D., Patilla, P. (1986) *Maths Explorer*. Glasgow: Collins (Six separate volumes for ages 5–11.)

Bulloch, I. (1995) *Action Maths*. London: Watts (Separate volumes for shapes, patterns, measure and games, all intended for use by parents.)

Child Education (1986) *Number Fun*. Leamington Spa: Scholastic Publications.

Coghill, J. (undated) *Help Your Child With Maths Games Pack*. London: BBC Publications.

Cornelius, M. and Parr, A. (1991) *What's Your Game?* Cambridge: Cambridge University Press.

Davis, J. and Tibbatts, S. (1995) *Teacher Timesavers Maths Puzzles*. Leamington Spa: Scholastic Publications.

De Bono, E. (1996) *Edward De Bono's Mind Pack*. London: Dorling Kindersley.

Dean, P. (1976) 'Commercial Games suitable for Middle and Secondary School Mathematics', in *Mathematics in School*, March 1976. (A list of about one hundred games and their suppliers.)

Diagram Visual Information Limited (1991) *Card Games*. Glasgow: HarperCollins (A Collins Gem.)

Diagram Visual Information Limited (1992) *Games for One*. Glasgow: HarperCollins (A Collins Gem.)

Edwards, R., Williams, A., Baggaley, P. (1993) *Number Activities and Games*. Stafford: NASEN Publications.

Erickson, T. (1989) *Get It Together: Math Problems for Groups, Grades 4–12*. Equals, Lawrence Hall of Science, Berkeley, California 94720 (ISBN 0912511532)

Fisher, A. and Gerster, G. *The Art of the Maze*. London: Weidenfeld & Nicolson.

Fraser, S. (1982) *Spaces: Solving Problems of Access to Careers in Engineering and Science*. Dale Seymour Publications, PO Box 10888, Palo Alto, California 94303, USA (ISBN 0866511474)

Golick, M. (1975) *Learning Through Card Games*. London: Wolfe Publishing, (ISBN 723406197)

Graham, A. T. (1985) *Help Your Child With Maths: A Guide For Parents*. Fontana (ISBN 0006368573)

Heimann, R. (1990) *Mind Bending Mazes*. London: Scholastic Publications (A Hippo book.)

Heimann, R. (1991) *Preposterous Puzzles*. London: Scholastic Publications (A Hippo book.)

Kirkby, D. (1992) *Games in the Teaching of Mathematics*. Cambridge: Cambridge University Press.

Kirkby, D. (1995) *Mini-Maths Series*. London: Heinemann (Separate volumes for numbers, patterns, shapes, measuring, sorting, number play.)

Langdon, N. and Snape, C. (1984) *A Way With Maths*. Cambridge: Cambridge University Press (ISBN 0521278833)

Langdon, N. and Cook, J. (1984) *Usborne Introduction To Maths*. London: Usborne.

The Mathematical Association (undated) *Fifty Per Cent Proof*. Gloucester: Stanley Thornes. Old Station Drive, Leckhampton, Cheltenham GL53 0DN

The Mathematical Association (1987) *Sharing Mathematics With Parents: Planning School-Based Events*. Stanley Thornes (ISBN 0859506959)

Merttens, R. (1987) *More Monster Maths*. London: Octopus.

Merttens, R. (1987) *Numbers Time and Money*. London: Octopus.
(The two items above are examples from the Parent and Child Programme, which includes a range of activity books and workbooks in mathematics.)

Merttens, R. and Leather, R. (1995a) *Impact: Holiday Activities*. Leamington Spa: Scholastic Publications.

Merttens, R. and Leather, R. (1995b) *Impact: Early Years Activities*. Leamington Spa: Scholastic Publications.

Merttens, R. and Leather, R. (1995c) *Impact: Shape – Key Stages 1 and 2*. Leamington Spa: Scholastic Publications.
(Many other IMPACT books exist, some fearsomely titled 'Impact Maths Homework'.)

Moscovich, I. (1984) *Supergames*. Hutchinson (ISBN 0091563814)

Moscovich, I. (1986) *Mind Benders: Games of Chance*. Penguin (ISBN 0140098240.) (Also see: *Games of Shape* ISBN 0140098259)

NES Arnold (see Appendix 2) (undated): *Multilink Traditional Games Pack*. (Ref SY 562/1.)

Owen, A. (1995) *Everyday Maths*. London: Wayland (Separate volumes for At Home, Ourselves, Fun With Food, Out and About.)

Pappas, T. (1989) *The Joy of Mathematics: Discovering Mathematics All Around You* 2nd edn. From Wide World Publishing or John Bibby Books, 1 Straylands Grove, York YO3 0EB. (ISBN 0933174659)

Parr, A. (undated) *Twenty-Five Mathematical Card Games*. The Longfield Press (see Appendix 2)

Rice, T. (1973) *Mathematical Games and Puzzles*. B & T Batsford. A book explaining more than forty types of puzzles and games. The final section deals with games for one or more players. Attractively set out. For primary school pupils upwards.

Sheppard, R. and Wilkinson, J. (1989) *The Strategy Games File*. Tarquin Publications (see Appendix 2) (ISBN 0906212707)

Sheppard, R. and Wilkinson, J. (1994) *Strategy Games*. Diss: Tarquin Publications.

Skemp, R.R. (1989) *Structured Activities for Primary Mathematics: How To Enjoy Real Mathematics*. London: Routledge. Volume 1 for the early years, volume 2 for the later years, volume 1a photomasters, volume 2b photomasters (designed for teacher use).

Smullyan, R. (1978) *What Is The Name of This Book?* London: Pelican.

Smullyan, R. (1990) *The Riddle of Dracula And Other Logical Puzzles*. London: Penguin (ISBN 0140135111)

Snape, C. and Scott, H. (1996a) *How Many?* Cambridge: Cambridge University Press.

Snape, C. and Scott, H. (1996b) *Puzzles, Mazes and Numbers*. Cambridge: Cambridge University Press.

Stenmark, J. K., Thompson, V., Cossey, R. (1986) *Family Math*. Equals, Lawrence Hall of Science, Berkeley, California 94720 (ISBN 0912511060)

Tapson, F. and Parr, A. (1979) *Pick A Pair*. London: A. & C. Black.

Tyler, J. and Round, G. (1980a) *Picture Puzzles*. London: Usborne (ISBN 0860204332)

Tyler, J. and Round, G. (1980b) *Number Puzzles*. London: Usborne (ISBN 0860204359)

Williams, M. and Somerwill, H. (1982) *Forty Maths Games To Make and Play*. Macmillan Education (ISBN 0333317300)

Dover Publications: New York – Books on mathematical and word recreations

W. S. Andrews, *Magic Squares and Cubes*.

S. Barr, *Mathematical Brain Benders*.

A. H. Beller, *Recreations in the Theory of Numbers*.

W. H. Benson and O. Jacoby, *Magic Cubes: New Recreations*.

W. H. Benson and O. Jacoby, *New Recreations with Magic Squares*.

H. W. Bergerson (ed.) *Palindromes and Anagrams*.

M. Brooke, *150 Puzzles in Crypto-arithmetic*.

L. Carroll, *Pillow Problems and a Tangled Tale*.

L. Carroll, *Symbolic Logic and the Game of Logic*.

H. S. M. Coxeter, *Regular Polytopes*.

H. E. Dudeney, *Amusements in Mathematics*.

A. Dunn (ed.) *Second Book of Mathematical Bafflers*.

A. R. Eckler, *Word Recreations*.

A. Friedland, *Puzzles in Math and Logic*.

J. Frohlichstein, *Mathematical Fun, Games and Puzzles*.

H. F. Gaines, *Crypto-analysis: A Study of Ciphers and their Solutions*.

M. Gardner, *Mathematics, Magic and Mystery*.

N. Gleason, *Cryptograms and Spygrams*.

L. A. Graham, *Ingenious Mathematical Problems and Methods*.

L. A. Graham, *The Surprise Attack in Mathematical Problems*.

R. V. Heath, *Mathemagic: Magic, Puzzles and Games with Numbers*.

R. Hufford, *Challenging Puzzles in Logic*.

J. A. H. Hunter, *Challenging Mathematical Teasers*.

J. A. H. Hunter, *Entertaining Mathematical Teasers and How to Solve Them*.

J. A. H. Hunter, *Fun with Figures*.

J. A. H. Hunter, *Mathematical Brain-Teasers*.

J. A. H. Hunter, *More Fun with Figures*.

J. A. H. Hunter and J. S. Madachy, *Mathematical Diversions*.

G. Kaufman, *New Word Puzzles*.

M. Kraitchik, *Mathematical Recreations*.

D. G. Wells, *Recreations in Logic*.

APPENDIX 4

List of software suppliers

In addition to regional centres supported by LEAs, the following are suppliers of software suitable for home use in the UK for various hardware platforms. Many will send catalogues on request.

ABLAC gives free telephone advice to parents and encourages home–school learning links – also has a catalogue – Tel. 01626 332233.
AVP, School Hill Centre, Chepstow, Monmouthshire NP6 5PH. Tel 01291 625439, fax 629671, email 100441.130@compuserve.com (primary catalogue and special needs catalogue).
Brilliant Computing. Tel. 01274 497617.
The British Library offers a catalogue of CD-ROMs. Tel. 0171 412 7797, email education@bl.uk.
Creative Curriculum Software. Tel. 01422 340524.
Don Johnston. Tel. 01925 241642.
Lander Software, 1 Atlantic Quay, Glasgow G2 8JE, freefone 0800 403040 or 0141 226 5611, fax 5622, email Lander@cix.compulink.co.uk.
The National Centre for Educational Technology (Tel. 01203 416994) also has much relevant information and are very helpful (email enquiry_desk@ncet.org.uk; also see their homepage at http://www.ncet.org.uk/). They produce a (long!) updated information sheeet on Educational Software Suppliers and a guide for parents called *Children's Software and Where To Get It*. They review CD-ROMs including those for mathematics and have a searchable software database.
New Media Tel. 0171 916 9999.
New Vision (CD-ROM only). Tel. 0181 964 3334.
Parents and Computers is a magazine for parents with children between 3 and 11 years. Tel. 01625 878888.
Parents' Information Network, PO Box 1577, London W7 3ZT. Tel. 0181 248 4666. http://www.pin–parents.com/
Rickitts Educational Media (REM), Great Western House, Langport, Somerset TA10 9YU. Tel. 01458 253636, fax 253646, email 100647.3472@compuserve.com. (Educational Software Yearbook, Special Needs Catalogue and CD-ROM catalogue.)
NW SEMERC. Tel. 0161 627 4469.
Sherston Software. Tel. 01666 840433.
Software Production Associates (SPA), PO Box 59, Tewkesbury GL20 6AB. Tel. 01684 833700, fax 833718, email sales@spasoft.demon.co.uk.
Tag Developments Ltd. Tel. 01474 357350.

APPENDIX 5

List of websites

The Internet is constantly changing, and readers are advised to conduct their own up-to-date search with the usual search engines. Listed below are some of the more enduring current websites, but even these may change.

There is a large number of locations dealing with mathematics, but most deal with teacher-directed mathematics in school, college or university. There are also websites which enable parents and children to rehearse major national mathematics tests (e.g. SATs). There are also sites which offer commercial profit-making services to parents (e.g. Water Street, The Digital

Education Network). Additionally, there are scores of email listservs and newsgroups for those interested in mathematics, but rarely for parents and children together. None of the above are listed below.

US Department of Education: Helping Your Child Learn Math
(in addition to a number of detailed activities, includes a listing of US resources for parents, books for children, and maths magazines and periodicals for adults and children)
http://www.ed.gov/pubs/parents/Math/index.html

Doing Mathematics With Your Child
(M. Hartog and P. Brosnan, 1994: ERIC Digest)
(US-based, brief general information, mentions some resources and projects, useful lists of and references to other parent guides and activities)
http://www.ericse.org/eric/digests/digest-m04.html

PRIME: Parent Resources in Mathematics Education
(M. Hartog and M. Reed: ERIC publication)
(a more extensive US-based annotated bibliography of parent guides, activities and programmes)
http://www.ericse.org/eric/publications/public-05.html

Family Math (The Berkeley EQUALS Programme)
(describes the programme, its email Newsletter, gives access to back issues of the newsletter, and contact details)
http://theory.lcs.mit.edu/~emjordan/famMath.html

Mathematics for Parents
(a series of newsletters for parents from the University of Wisconsin Center for Educational Research, each dealing with a specific area of maths)
http://www.wcer.wisc.edu/Projects/Mathematics_and_Science/Modeling_in_Math_and_Scie
nce/Newsletters/Table_of_Contents.html

Mathematics Resources for Parents
(brief list with price, contact details; some emphasis on materials also in Spanish)
http://www.iusd.k12.ca.us/curriculum/mathrsrc.htm

'Math Resources'
(indexes a number of other sites, including: a gallery of interactive geometry, math magic, geometry newsgroups (if you can't figure out the answer, someone else in the world probably can!), Mega-Math, Fun Math, Ask Dr Math, and so on)
http://www.teleport.com/~vincer/math.html

Ask Dr Math
(provides a solving service for K-12 maths problems, among other things)
http://forum.swarthmore.edu/dr.math/

Mathmania
(from the Canadian Mathematical Society, exploring the frontiers of mathematics, particularly via knots, graphs, sorting networks and finite state machines)
http://csr.uvic.ca/~mmania/

Parents' mathematical library – bibliography

ACE Information Sheet
Parents And Maths
Advisory Centre for Education, 18 Victoria Park Square, London E2 9PB 4 pages
Rosemarie Brewer and Marion Cranmer (1988)
Bright Ideas – Maths Games
Scholastic Publications Ltd, Marlborough House, Holly Walk, Leamington Spa, Warwickshire CV32 4LS (ISBN 0590708740) 127 pages

Avelyn Davidson (1983)
Maths and Me
Shortland Publications Ltd, re-published 1988 by NES Arnold (see Appendix 2) (ISBN 0560091001) 40 pages

GEMS
A Parent's Guide to Great Explorations in Math and Science.
Berkeley CA: Lawrence Hall of Science.

Alan T. Graham (1985)
Help Your Child With Maths: A Guide for Parents.
London: Fontana.

Rose Griffiths (1988)
Maths Through Play
MacDonald & Co (Publishers) Ltd, Greater London House, Hampstead Road, London NW1 7QX (ISBN 0356134601) 96 pages

Ruth Merttens
Parent and Child Programme
Octopus Publishing Group Ltd, Michelin House, 81 Fulham Road, London SW3 6RB
a) *Counting On* – 1987 (ISBN 1852700092) 32 pages
b) *Beginning to Count (1)* – 1987 (ISBN 1852700084) 32 pages
c) *Beginning to Count (2)* – 1988 (ISBN 1852700645) 32 pages
d) *Parents' Guide to Your Child's Maths* – 1988 (ISBN 1852700599) 32 pages
e) *Fun With Shape* – 1987 (ISBN 1852700203) 32 pages

Frances Mosley and Susan Meredith (1989)
Help Your Child Learn Number Skills
Usborne Publishing, 20 Garrick Street, London WC2E 9BJ (ISBN 0746003145) 48 pages

Angela Walsh (ed.) (1988)
Help Your Child With Maths – BBC TV Series
BBC Books, BBC Enterprises Ltd, Woodlands, 80 Wood Lane, London W12 OTT (ISBN 0563214449) 128 pages

Further reading for parents of preschool children

C. Heald and V. Eustice (1988)
Ready for Maths
Hippo Books, Scholastic Publications (ISBN 0590709534)

Dorothy M. Jeffree (1989)
Let Me Count
London: Souvenir Press (ISBN 0285650815)

J. Millman and P. Behrmann (1979)
Parents as Playmates
Human Sciences Press, 3 Henrietta Street, London WC2E 8LU (ISBN 0877054045)

J. Mokros, (1996)
Beyond Facts and Flashcards: Exploring Math with Your Kids.
Portsmouth NH: Heinemann.

APPENDIX 7

Further reading for professionals

Apelman, M. & King, J. (1989) *Pizzas, Pennies and Pumpkin Seeds: Mathematical Activities for Parents and Children*. Denver CO: State Department of Education. ERIC ED327395.
Campbell, P. B. (1992) *Maths, Science and Your Daughter: What Can Parents Do?* Washington DC: US Department of Education (ERIC ED350172).
Centre for Mathematics Education (1995) *An ABC of Number*. Milton Keynes: Open University Press.
Neil, M.S. (1994) *Parent–Teacher Partnerships: Enhancing Learning in Mathematics*. Georgia. ERIC ED377054.
O'Connell, S.R. (1992) 'Math pairs: parents as partners', *Arithmetic Teacher* **40** (1), 10–12.
Struggle: Mathematics for Low Attainers. Journal for teachers produced by The Mathematical Association, 259 London Road, Leicester LE2 3BE Tel. 703877.
It may be worth contacting The National Centre for Literacy and Numeracy, London House, 59–65 London Street, Reading RG1 4EW Tel. 01189 527500.

References

Askew, M. and Wiliam, D. (1995) *Recent Research in Mathematics Education 5–16*. London: HMSO.

Basic Skills Agency (1997) *International Numeracy Survey: A Comparison of the Basic Numeracy Skills of Adults 16–60 in Seven Countries*. London: Basic Skills Agency.

Beasley, J. (1990) *The Mathematics of Games*. Oxford: Oxford University Press.

Bentz, J. L. and Fuchs, L. S. (1996) 'Improving peers helping behavior to students with learning disabilities during mathematics peer tutoring', *Learning Disability Quarterly* **19**(4), 202–15.

Beyer, A. (1993) 'Assessing students' performance using observations, reflections and other methods', in Webb, N. and Coxford, A. (eds) *Assessment in the Mathematics Classroom*. Reston VA: National Council of Teachers of Mathematics.

Bower, T. (1981) 'Cognitive development', in Roberts, M. and Tamburrini, J. (eds) *Child Development 0–5*. Edinburgh: Holmes McDougall.

Brainerd, C. J. (1978) *Piaget's Theory of Intelligence*. Englewood Cliffs, NJ: Prentice-Hall.

Brandon, P. R. *et al.* (1987) 'Children's mathematics achievement in Hawaii: sex differences favoring girls', *American Educational Research Journal* **24**(3), 437–61.

Britz, M. W. *et al.* (1989) 'The effects of peer tutoring on mathematics performance: a recent review', *B. C. Journal of Special Education* **13**(1), 17–33.

Brodsky, S. *et al.* (1994) *An Urban Family Math Collaborative*. New York: Center for Advanced Study in Education, City University of New York. ERIC Document Reproduction Service No., ED379154.

Brown, B. W. (1991) 'How gender and socioeconomic status affect reading and mathematics achievement', *Economics of Education Review* **10**(4), 343–57.

Bruner, J. S. (1960) *The Process of Education*. Cambridge MA: Harvard University Press.

Bruner, J. S. (1966) *Towards a Theory of Instruction*. Cambridge MA: Harvard University Press.

Bruner, J. S. (1971) *The Relevance of Education*. London: Allen & Unwin.

Burrett, A. R. (1968) 'Number games as an aid to the development of basic mathematical concepts', *Primary Mathematics* **6**(3), 14–22.

Bynner, J. and Parsons, S. (1997) *Does Numeracy Matter? Evidence from the National Child Development Study on the Impact of Poor Numeracy on Adult Life*. London: Basic Skills Unit & Avanti Books.

Campbell, P. B. (1992) *Math, Science, and Your Daughter: What Can Parents Do?* Washington DC: US Department of Education. ERIC Document Reproduction Service No. ED 350172.

Campbell, P. (1995) `Redefining the 'girl problem in mathematics'', in Secada, W., Fennema, E. and Adajian, L. (eds) *New Directions for Equity in Mathematics Education*. Cambridge: Cambridge University Press.

Carpenter, B., Moore, J. and Lindoe, S. (1991) 'Changing attitudes', in Tilstone, C. (ed.) *Teaching Pupils with Severe Learning Difficulties*. London: David Fulton Publishers.

Chambers, T., Mountain, M. and Wood, D. (1992) *Parental Involvement in Science: Science Co-*

ordinator Pack. Hull: Humberside County Council Education Department.

Choat, E. (1981) 'Primary mathematics and psychology', *Journal of the Association of Educational Psychologists* **5**(7), 17–23.

Clive, D. (1989) 'Puzzling over maths', *Special Children*, January, 18–19.

Cockcroft, W.H. (1982) *Mathematics Counts: Report of the Committee of Enquiry into the Teaching of Mathematics in Schools*. London: HMSO.

Cohen, P. A., Kulik, J. A. and Kulik, C-L. C. (1982) 'Educational outcomes of tutoring: a meta-analysis of findings', *American Educational Research Journal* **19**(2), 237–48.

COGNET (1991) *COGNET Follow Through Education Model Research Report: Studies of Impact on Children, Teachers and Parents, 1988–1991*. Nashville TN: Cognitive Enrichment Network. ERIC Document Reproduction Service No. ED343720.

Cornelius, M. and Parr, A. (1991) *What's Your Game?* Cambridge: Cambridge University Press.

Costello, P. *et al.* (1991) *Sharing Maths Learning with Children – A Guide for Parents, Teachers and Others*. ERIC Document Reproduction Service No. ED364402.

Daniels, H. and Anghileri, J. (1995) *Secondary Mathematics and Special Educational Needs*. London: Cassell.

Davidson, N. (1985) 'Small group learning in mathematics', in Slavin, R. *et al.* (eds) *Learning to Cooperate, Cooperating to Learn*. New York: Plenum Press.

Davidson, N. (1989) 'Cooperative learning and mathematics achievement: a research review', *Cooperative Learning* **10**(2), 15–16.

Davidson, N. (ed.) (1990) *Cooperative Learning in Mathematics: A Handbook for Teachers*. Menlo Park CA: Addison-Wesley.

Davidson, N. and Kroll, D. L. (1991) 'An overview of research on cooperative learning related to mathematics', *Journal for Research in Mathematics Education* **22**(5), 362–65.

Dean, P. G. (1978) 'A study of the use of mathematical games in the primary school', in Megarry, J. (ed.) *Perspectives on Academic Gaming & Simulation 1 & 2*. London: Kogan Page; New York: Nichols.

Dees, R. *et al.* (1989) 'Cooperative mathematics lesson plans', *Cooperative Learning* **10**(2), 32–40.

Department for Education and Employment (1995) *Mathematics in the National Curriculum*. London: HMSO.

Dickens, M. N. and Cornell, D. G. (1990) *Parental Influences on the Mathematics Self-concept of High-achieving Adolescent Girls*. Charleston W VA: Appalachia Educational Lab. ERIC Document Reproduction Service No. ED318207.

Donaldson, M. (1978) *Children's Minds*. Glasgow: Collins/Fontana.

Duren, P. E. (1992) 'The effects of cooperative group work versus independent practice on the learning of some problem-solving strategies', *School Science and Mathematics* **92**(2), 80–83.

Durkin, K. (1993) 'The representations of number in infancy and early childhood', in Pratt, C. and Garton, A. F. (eds) *Systems of Representation in Children: Development and Use*. Chichester: Wiley.

Durkin, K. and Shire, B. (1991) *Language in Mathematical Education: Research and Practice*. Milton Keynes: Open University Press.

East Sussex County Council (1990) *Does It Add Up?: National Curriculum Guidelines for Severe Learning Difficulty Schools*. Hove: East Sussex LEA.

Fantuzzo, J. W. *et al.* (1992) 'Effects of reciprocal peer tutoring on mathematics and school adjustment: a component analysis', *Journal of Educational Psychology* **84**(3), 331–9.

Fantuzzo, J. W., Davis, G. Y. and Ginsburg, M. D. (1995) 'Effects of parent involvement in isolation or in combination with peer tutoring on student self-concept and mathematics achievement', *Journal of Educational Psychology* **87**(2), 272–81.

Fennema, E. and Sherman, J. (1978) 'Sex-related differences in mathematics achievement and related factors: a further study', *Journal for Research in Mathematics Education* **9**(3), 189–203.

Fennema, E. and Meyer, M. (1989) 'Gender, equity and mathematics', in Secada, W. (ed.) *Equity in Education*. London: Falmer Press.

Foxman, D. (1992) *Learning Mathematics and Science: The Second International Assessment of Educational Progress in England.* Slough: NFER.

Franca, V. M. *et al.* (1990) 'Peer tutoring among behaviorally disordered students: academic and social benefits to tutor and tutee', *Education and Treatment of Children* **13**(2), 109–128.

Fuchs, L.S. *et al.* (1994) 'The nature of student interactions during peer tutoring with and without prior training and experience', *American Educational Research Journal* **31**(1), 75–103.

Gelman, R. and Gallistel, C. R. (1978) *The Child's Understanding of Number.* Cambridge MA: Harvard University Press.

GEMS (1991) *A Parent's Guide to Great Explorations in Math and Science.* Berkeley CA: Lawrence Hall of Science.

George, M. and Mosley, F. (1988) 'Making fun of maths', *Special Children*, April, 22–3.

Goldberg, S. (1990) *Developing and Implementing a Parental Awareness Program to Enhance Children's Mathematics Performance and Attitude.* ERIC Document Reproduction Service No. ED327383.

Graham, A. T. (1985) *Help Your Child With Maths: A Guide for Parents.* London: Fontana/Collins.

Graves, N. and Graves, T. (eds) (1991) 'Cooperative Learning and Science'. Special issue of *Cooperative Learning* **11**(3). Santa Cruz CA: International Association for the Study of Co-operation in Education.

Greenwood, C. R. (1991) 'Classwide peer tutoring: longitudinal effects on the reading, language, and mathematics achievement of at-risk students', *Journal of Reading, Writing, and Learning Disabilities International* **7**(2), 105–123.

Hanna, G. (1989) 'Mathematics achievement of girls and boys in grade eight: results from twenty countries', *Educational Studies in Mathematics* **20**(2), 225–232.

Heller, L. R. and Fantuzzo, J. W. (1993) 'Reciprocal peer tutoring and parent partnership: does parent involvement make a difference?' *School Psychology Review*, **22**(3), 517–34.

Hughes, M. (1983) 'Teaching arithmetic to pre-school children', *Educational Review* **35**(2), 163–73.

Hughes, M. (1986) *Children and Number: Difficulties in Learning Mathematics.* Oxford: Blackwell.

Hyde, J. S. *et al.* (1990) 'Gender comparisons of mathematics attitudes and affect: a meta-analysis', *Psychology of Women Quarterly* **14**(3), 299–324.

Jasmine, G. and Jasmine, J. (1996) *Activities for Math: Cooperative Learning Lessons.* Huntington Beach CA: Teacher Created Materials Inc.

Jayaratne, T. E. (1987) *The Impact of Mothers' Math Experiences on Their Daughters' Attitudes Toward Math.* ERIC Document Reproduction Service No. ED297967.

Jeffree, D. M. (1989) *Let Me Count.* London: Souvenir Press.

Jennings, D. (1983) 'Mathematics in the secondary school: a programme of support involving parents', *Remedial Education* **18**(4), 171–3.

Johnson, D. W. and Johnson, R. T. (1991) *Learning Together and Alone.* Needham Heights MA: Allyn and Bacon.

Jones, K. and Haylock, D. W. (1985) 'Developing children's understanding in mathematics', *Remedial Education* **20**(1), 30–34.

Judd, C. M., Smith, E. R. and Kidder, L. H. (1991) *Research Methods in Social Relations*, 6th edn. Fort Worth TX: Holt, Rinehart and Winston.

Kanter, P. F., Dorfman, C. and Hearn, E. (1992) *Helping Your Child Learn Math with Activities for Children Aged 5 Through 13.* Washington DC: Office of Educational Research and Improvement. ERIC Document Reproduction Service No. ED355122.

Kirkby, D. (1992) *Games in the Teaching of Mathematics.* Cambridge: Cambridge University Press.

Kohr, R. L. *et al.* (1989) 'The relationship of race, class and gender with mathematics achievement for fifth-, eighth-, and eleventh-grade students in Pennsylvania schools', *Peabody Journal of Education* **66**(2), 141–71.

Kwok, D. C. and Lytton, H. (1996) 'Perceptions of mathematics ability versus actual mathematics performance in Canadian and Hong Kong children', *British Journal of Educational Psychology* **66**(2), 209–222.

Kyriacou, C. (1991) 'Small group work in secondary school mathematics', *Mathematics in School* **20**(3), 44–6.

Leder, G. (1990) 'Gender and classroom practice', in Burton, L. (ed.) *Gender and Mathematics: An International Perspective*. London: Cassell Educational.

Leonard, L. M. and Tracy, D. M. (1993) 'Using games to meet the standards for middle school students', *Arithmetic Teacher* **40**(9), 499–503.

Leutzinger, L., Bertheau, M. and Nanke, G. (1993) 'A day in the life of an elementary school mathematics classroom: assessment in action', in Webb, N. and Coxford, A. (eds) *Assessment in the Mathematics Classroom*. Reston VA: National Council of Teachers of Mathematics.

Light, P. (1986) 'Context, conservation and conversation', in Richards, M. and Light, P. (eds) *Children of Social Worlds*. Cambridge: Polity Press.

McConkey, R. (1987) 'Interaction: the name of the game', in Smith, B. (ed.) *Interactive Approaches to the Education of Children with Severe Learning Difficulties*. Birmingham: Westhill College.

McConkey, R. and McEvoy, J. (1986) 'Games for learning to count', *British Journal of Special Education* **13**(2), 59–62.

Manchester Teacher Fellows (1993) *Mathematics For All*. London: David Fulton Publishers.

Manger, T. (1995) 'Gender differences in mathematical achievement at the Norwegian elementary school level', *Scandinavian Journal of Educational Research*, **39**(3), 257–69.

Martin, S. (1993) *KnapSack Math*. Boston MA: World Education Inc. ERIC Document Reproduction Service No. ED394019.

Merttens, R. and Vass, J. (1987) 'Parents in schools: raising money or raising standards?' *Education 3–13*, June, 23–27.

Merttens, R. and Vass, J. (eds) (1993) *Partnerships in Maths: Parents and Schools – The IMPACT Project*. London and Washington DC: Falmer Press.

Mevarech, Z. R. (1985) 'The effects of cooperative mastery learning strategies on mathematical achievement', *Journal of Educational Research* **78**(6), 372–7.

Mokros, J. (1996) *Beyond Facts and Flashcards: Exploring Math with Your Kids*. Portsmouth NH: Heinemann.

Mulryan, C. M. (1992) 'Student passivity during cooperative small groups in mathematics', *Journal of Educational Research* **85**(5), 261–73.

Nattiv, A. (1994) 'Helping behaviors and math achievement gain of students using cooperative learning', *Elementary School Journal* **94**(3), 285–97.

Neil, M. S. (1994) *Parent–Teacher Partnerships: Enhancing Learning in Mathematics*. ERIC Document Reproduction Service No. ED377054.

Neilan, A. and Currie, L. (1994) 'Adding parents to the equation: 5–14 mathematics curriculum + parental involvement = development of early number skills', in Scottish Office Education Department, *Professional Development Initiatives 1992–3*. Edinburgh: Scottish Office Education Department.

Neumark, V. (1997) 'Games pupils play', *Times Educational Supplement* May 23 1997, Extra Mathematics, IV.

Nichols, J. D. and Hall, N. (1995) *The Effects of Cooperative Learning on Student Achievement and Motivation in a High School Geometry Class*. ERIC Document Reproduction Service No. ED387341.

Nunes, T., Schliemann, A. D. and Carraher, D. W. (1993) *Street Mathematics and School Mathematics*. Cambridge: Cambridge University Press.

Nunes, T. and Bryant, P. (1996) *Children Doing Mathematics*. Oxford and Cambridge MA: Blackwell.

Onslow, B. (1992) 'Improving the attitude of students and parents through family involvement in mathematics', *Mathematics Education Research Journal* **4**(3), 24–31.

Orton, A. and Frobisher, L. (1996) *Insights into Teaching Mathematics*. London: Cassell.

Osguthorpe, R. T. and Scruggs, T. E. (1990) 'Special education students as tutors: a review and analysis', in Goodlad, S. and Hirst, B. (eds) *Explorations in Peer Tutoring*. Oxford: Blackwell.

Owens, V. W. (1992) *Create a Math Environment. A Parent-Helper Book for Those Who Want Arithmetic Made Touchable.* ERIC Document Reproduction Service No. ED372916.

Paskin, J. (1986) 'Families' Understanding of Number and Games: Parental Involvement in Mathematical Education'. Unpublished MSc Educational Psychology dissertation, University of Sheffield.

Perry, J. and Simmons, K. (1987) "Shared Maths': a successful home-school project', *Support for Learning* 2(2), 9–12.

Phillips, N. B. *et al.* (1993) 'Combining classwide curriculum-based measurement and peer tutoring to help general educators provide adaptive education', *Learning Disabilities Research and Practice* 8(3), 148–56.

Piaget, J. (1952) *The Child's Conception of Number.* London: Routledge and Kegan Paul.

Pimm, D. (1991) `Communicating mathematically', in Durkin, K. and Shire, B. (eds) *Language in Mathematical Education: Research and Practice.* Milton Keynes: Open University Press.

Pratt, S. J. and Moesner, C. (1990) *A Comparative Study of Traditional and Cooperative Learning on Student Achievement.* ERIC Document Reproduction Service No. ED325258.

Raines, L. (1988) 'Parental attitudes to maths: a primary school survey', British Psychological Society, Division of Educational and Child Psychology Newsletter **32**, 6–8.

Reid, J. (1992) *The Effects of Cooperative Learning with Intergroup Competition on the Math Achievement of Seventh Grade Students.* ERIC Document Reproduction Service No. ED355106.

Rillero, P. (1994) *Doing Science With Your Children.* (ERIC Digest EDO-SE-94-1). Columbus OH: ERIC Clearinghouse for Science, Mathematics and Environmental Education.

Risk, D. (1988) 'An Evaluation of Parental Involvement in Mathematics'. Unpublished MSc Educational Psychology dissertation, University of Manchester.

Robbins, B. (1991) 'Mathematics for all', in Ashdown, R. *et al.* (eds) *The Curriculum Challenge: Access to the National Curriculum for Pupils with Learning Difficulties.* London: Falmer Press.

Robertson, A.H. *et al.* (1983) *QUEST: Screening, Diagnostic and Remediation Kit.* Walton-on-Thames: Nelson.

Rogers, P. J. and Miller, J. V. (1984) 'Playway mathematics: theory, practice and some results', *Educational Research* **26**(3), 200–207.

Scottish Office Education and Industry Department (SOEID) (1996a) *Achievements of Secondary 1 and Secondary 2 Pupils in Mathematics and Science: Third International Mathematics and Science Study.* Edinburgh: SOEID.

Scottish Office Education and Industry Department (SOEID) (1996b) *Assessment of Achievement Programme: Mathematics 1994.* Edinburgh: SOEID.

Scruggs, T. and Mastropieri, M. (1997) 'Tutoring and students with special needs,' in Topping, K. J. and Ehly, S. (eds), *Peer Assisted Learning.* Mahwah NJ and London: Lawrence Erlbaum.

Sears, N. C. and Medearis, L. (1992) *Natural Math: A Progress Report on Implementation of a Family Involvement Project for Early Childhood Mathematics among Children of the Oklahoma Seminole Head Start and Boley Head Start.* ERIC Document Reproduction Service No. ED352172.

Sears, N. C. and Medearis, L. (1993) *Educating Teachers for Family Involvement with Young Native Americans.* ERIC Document Reproduction Service No. ED367513.

Sebba, J., Byers, R. and Rose, R. (1993) *Redefining the Whole Curriculum for Pupils with Learning Difficulties.* London: David Fulton Publishers.

Sedlacek, D. S. (1990) *Mathematics Achievement and Classroom Instructional Activities: National Assessment of Educational Progress 1985–86.* Washington DC: National Center for Educational Statistics. ERIC Document Reproduction Service No.ED326445.

Sharp, R. *et al.* (1995) *Scribble Scrabble: Ready-in-a-Minute Math Games.* ERIC Document Reproduction Service No. ED387358.

Sharpley, A. M. and Sharpley, C. F. (1981) 'Peer tutoring: a review of the literature', *Collected Original Resources in Education (CORE)* 5(3), 7–C11 (fiche 7 & 8).

Skemp, R. R. (1971) *The Psychology of Learning Mathematics.* Harmondsworth: Penguin.

Skemp, R. R. (1978) *Intelligence, Learning and Action.* Chichester: Wiley.

Skemp R. R. (1989a) *Mathematics in the Primary School*. London: Routledge.

Skemp, R. R. (1989b) *Structured Activities for Primary Mathematics: How To Enjoy Real Mathematics*. London: Routledge.

Slavin, R. E. (1985) 'Effects of whole class, ability grouped, and individualized instruction on mathematics achievement', *American Educational Research Journal* **22**(3), 351–67.

Slavin, R. E. (1990) *Cooperative Learning: Theory, Research and Practice*. Englewood Cliffs NJ: Prentice Hall.

Solomon, J. and Lee, J. (1991) 'Experimenting at home', *Child Education* **68**(8), 36–7.

Stocking, V. B. and Goldstein, D. (1992) *Course Selection and Performance of Very High Ability Students: Is There a Gender Gap?* ERIC Document Reproduction Service No. ED372019.

Tartre, L. A. and Fennema, E. (1995) 'Mathematics achievement and gender: a longitudinal study of selected cognitive and affective variables grades 6–12', *Educational Studies in Mathematics* **28**(3), 199–217.

Topping, K. J. (1988) *The Peer Tutoring Handbook: Promoting Cooperative Learning*. London: Croom Helm; Cambridge MA: Brookline.

Topping, K. J. (1992) 'Cooperative learning and peer tutoring: an overview', *The Psychologist* **5**(4), 151–7.

Topping, K. J. (1995) *Paired Reading, Spelling and Writing: The Handbook for Teachers and Parents*. London and New York: Cassell.

Topping, K. J. (1998) *The Paired Science Handbook: Parental Involvement and Peer Tutoring in Science*. London: David Fulton Publishers; Bristol PA: Taylor and Francis.

Topping, K. J. and Wolfendale, S. W. (eds) (1985) *Parental Involvement in Children's Reading*. London: Croom Helm; New York: Nichols.

Topping, K. J. and Bamford, J. (1990) *Paired Maths at Deighton High School: Evaluative Feedback*. Huddersfield: Kirklees Psychological Service.

Topping, K.J. and Bamford, J. (1998) *The Paired Maths Handbook: Parental Involvement and Peer Tutoring in Mathematics*. London: David Fulton Publishers; Bristol PA: Taylor & Francis

Topping, K. J. and Whiteley, M. (1993) 'Sex differences in the effectiveness of peer tutoring', *School Psychology International* **14**(1), 57–67.

Topping, K. J. and Ehly, S. (eds) (1998) *Peer Assisted Learning*. Mahwah NJ and London: Erlbaum.

Urion, D. K. (1992) 'Student achievement in small-group instruction versus teacher-centered instruction in mathematics', *Primus* **2**(3), 257–65.

Valentine, D. (1992) *Educational Play: Mathematics. Games and Activities to Stimulate Your Child in Mathematics*. Unionville NY: Royal Fireworks Printing Co.

Vygotsky, L. S. (1962) *Thought and Language*. Cambridge MA: MIT Press.

Vygotsky, L. S. (1978) *Mind in Society*. Cambridge MA: Harvard University Press.

Webb, N. (1985) 'Student interaction and learning in small groups', in Slavin, R. *et al.* (eds) *Learning to Cooperate, Cooperating to Learn*. New York: Plenum Press.

Webb, N. M. (1991) 'Task-related verbal interaction and mathematics learning in small groups', *Journal for Research in Mathematics Education* **22**(5), 366–89.

Whitebread, D. (1995) 'Emergent mathematicians, or how to help young children become confident mathematicians', in Anghileri, J. (ed.) *Children's Mathematical Thinking in the Primary Years*. London: Cassell.

Wolfendale, S. W. and Topping, K. J. (eds) (1996) *Family Involvement in Literacy: Effective Partnerships in Education*. London and New York: Cassell.

Wood, D. (1988) *How Children Think and Learn*. Oxford: Blackwell.

Wood, D. and O'Malley, C. (1996) 'Collaborative learning between peers: an overview', *Educational Psychology in Practice* **11**(4), 4–9.

Woolgar, J. (1986) 'Learning how to "count us in"', *British Journal of Special Education* **13**(4), 147–50.

Young, E. and Young, B. (1991) *Help Your Child With Science*. Cambridge: Cambridge University Press.

Subject and author index

Activity Sheets 18, 28, 29, 30, 34, 35, 36, 39, 40, 41, 69
adaptability 7
American Chemical Society 19, 52
Askew, M. 4, 47, 65
assessment
   maths 54–5, 56, 64, 65, 66–8, 75–6, 79, 81
   science 70
'Assessment Activities in Mathematics' (Duncan and Mitchell) 67
Assessment of Achievement Programme (Scottish Office) 4
attitudes
   to maths 3–4, 16, 32, 37–8, 63, 76, 79, 81
   to science 32, 37, 63, 70
Australia 13, 19, 52

badges 41
'Basic Number Diagnostic Test' (Gillham) 67
Beasley, J. 22, 45
behaviour, interactive 87
Bentz, J.L. 48
Beyer, A. 64
bonds 26, 27, 86, 95–6
books
   games/puzzle 101–4
   for parents 105–7
boys 4, 5, 17–18, 61, 79, 81, 82 *see also* gender

Brandon, P.R. 5
Britain *see* UK/Britain
Britz, M.W. 48
Brodsky, S. 50
Broom Nursery Project 61
Brown, B.W. 5
Bruner, Jerome 7, 45
Bryant, P 7

Canada 13, 38, 49 *see also* North America
cards 23
Carmichael 72
cataloguing 35–6
CATCH criterion-referenced screening battery 66–7
Cheyne 14
classroom
   cooperative learning and peer tutoring in 71–82
   maths games in 44–6, 71–5, 76–8, 79–81, 82
   observation in Paired Science 70
   see also Special Needs
Classwide Peer Tutoring (CWPT) model 48
Clive, D. 51
Cockcroft Report (1982) 2, 3, 28, 44, 56, 65, 75
COGNET (Cognitive Enrichment Network) Follow Through project 49
cognitive conflict 6, 18

colour-coding 35–6
computation 27
computers 91-2 *see also* Internet
concept formation 9
concepts, learning of 9, 20
conservation 24, 25, 26, 87, 94
consultations, initial 32–4
cooperative/collaborative learning 6,
    11–12, 18, 46–8, 71–82, 91
Cornelius, M. 45, 74
Costello, P. 13
counting 24, 25, 26, 27, 86, 87, 94
criterion-referenced tests 56, 65, 66–7, 69,
    75–6
cross-school peer-tutoring 83–8
Currie, L. 51
CWPT (Classwide peer tutoring) model
    48

Davidson, Neil 11, 46, 47
Dean, P.G. 45
Dees, R. 12
diagnostic tests 56, 57, 58, 65, 67–8, 69
disabled children 46
discussion 8, 9–10, 81
display 35–6, 73–4
Durkin, K 9, 21

'Early Mathematics Concepts'
    (EMC; Ashby, Ruddock and Sizmur)
    67–8
'Early Mathematics Diagnostic Kit'
    (Lumb and Lumb) 67
Eastern Europe 2
England 2, 17–18 *see also* UK/Britain
Equal Opportunies Commission 13
ERIC Clearinghouse for Science,
    Mathematics and Environmental
    Education 92
'Eureka' 4
evaluation
    methods 41–2, 62–70, 75–6
    of classroom Paired Maths project
    76–82

of cross-school project 88
of Paired Maths in Kirklees 53–60
of Paired Science projects 60–61
of practices related to Paired Maths
    41–52
of practices related to Paired Science
    52

everyday life, maths in 1, 2
exchange system, games 36, 57
extension games 26, 27, 99–100

'Family Math' programme 13, 49, 50
Fantuzzo, John 48, 49
feedback 41–2
5–14 Curriculum (Scotland) 3, 44, 72, 75
follow-up meeting 41–3
Franca, V.M. 48
Frobisher, L. 65
Fuchs, L.S. 48

games, mathematical
    classroom use 44–6, 71–5, 76–8, 79–81,
    82
    display and cataloguing 35–6, 73–4
    exchange system 36, 57
    and Key Stages 24–7, 94–100
    and Paired Maths projects 15, 16, 21–2,
    34, 35–6, 38–9, 40, 41, 57, 59, 71–5, 76–8,
    79–81, 82
    and 'Play Along Maths' 14
    principles and rationale behind use of
    6–7, 10–11, 20–22, 37–9
    rules 74, 76–7, 80
    selecting 22–3
    sources of 27–8, 73, 100–103
    and special needs 84, 86–7
GEMS (Great Explorations in Math and
    Science) programme 19, 52
gender 4–5, 17–18, 61, 79, 81–2 *see also*
    boys; girls; men; mothers; women
girls 4, 5, 17–18, 47, 61, 74, 79, 81, 82 *see
    also* gender
Goldberg, S. 12–13
Graham, Alan 13

Great Explorations in Math and Science (GEMS) programme 19, 52
Greenwood, Charles 48
'Group Mathematics Tests' (Young) 66

habit-learning 7
Hall, N. 47
handling data 24
Hawaii 5
Hawthorne Effect 82
Haylock, D.W. 9
head teacher 31
Heller, L.R. 49
Highfields special school 84–8
Hong Kong 2, 38
Hughes, M. 7, 45
Humberside County Council 19, 52

IMPACT project 13–14, 18, 19, 52
in-service training 15
infants, Paired Maths projects with 53–5, 56, 57
integration 83
interactive behaviour 87
Internet 91–2, 104–5
interview schedules 56, 65, 67–8

Japan 2, 3
Jasmine, G. and J. 11
Jeffree, Dorothy 84
Jennings, D. 13, 50
Johnson, D.W. and R.T. 47, 74
Jones, K. 9
juniors see primary school children

Kanter, P.F. 13
Key Stage 1 15, 20, 22, 24–6, 94–6
Key Stage 2 15, 20, 26, 96–7
Key Stage 3 15, 20, 26–7, 97–100
key words 18, 29, 70
Kirklees
    Paired Maths in 53–60
    Psychological Service 14
Korea 2

Kroll, D.L. 46, 47

language
    in maths 9–10, 24, 25, 38, 40
    in science 18, 29, 38, 40 see also key words
launch meeting 37–41
leaflets 40
learning 5-9 see also concept formation; cooperative/collaborative learning
Learning Mathematics and Science. The Second International Assessment of Educational Progress in England (Foxman) 2
Leder, G. 5
Leutzinger, L. 64
Likert scale 76
logic 73

McConkey, Roy 46, 84
McEvoy, J. 46, 84
Makaton 83, 84, 85
Martin, S. 13
matching 24, 25, 26, 86, 95–6
'Math Resources' website 92
mathematics
    attitudes to 3–4, 16, 32, 37–8, 63, 76, 79, 81
    cooperative learning in 11–12, 46–8, 71–82
    curriculum 2, 3, 20, 22–3, 24, 26, 27, 44, 72, 86
    discussion in 8, 9–10, 81
    games see games, mathematical
    language 9–10, 25, 38
    learning 5–9, 20
    parental involvement in 10, 12–14, 14–15, 21, 49–52, 53–4, 59, 63, 69
    peer tutoring in 12, 48–9, 71–82, 83–8
    standards 2–3
    tests see tests
    usefulness and importance of 1–2
    see also Paired Maths
'Mathematics for Parents' electronic

newsletters 91–2
MATHS *see* Multiply Attainments
  Through Home Support Project
measurement 27
meetings
  consultation 32–3
  follow-up 41–3
  launch 37–41
  pre-project 57
men 1 *see also* gender
Miller, J.V. 45
Millers Neuk Project 60–61
Moesner, C. 47
Mokros, J. 13
Money 73, 74
monitors 74, 80–81
mothers 5, 70 *see also* women
movement 73, 74, 77
Multiply Attainments Through Home
  Support (Paired Maths pilot project)
  14, 53–5

National Child Development Study 1
National Curriculum 2, 3, 20, 22–3, 24,
  26, 27, 29, 44, 65, 69, 72, 83, 86
'Natural Math' programme 13, 49–50
Neil, M.S. 13
Neilan, A. 51
Neumark, V. 72
Nichols, J.D. 47
norm-referenced tests 56, 65, 66, 69, 75
North America 11, 12–13, 49–50 *see also*
  Canada; USA
North Manchester Mathematics Centre
  (NORMAC) 28
Norwegians 5
number 22–3, 24, 26, 27, 73, 74, 77, 96, 99
numeracy skills, importance of 1
Nunes, T. 2, 7

objectives 31–2
observation schedules 56, 65, 67–8
O'Malley, C. 47
Onslow, B. 13, 49

'Operation Smart' 4–5
ordering 24, 25, 26, 27, 87, 95
Orton, A. 65
outcomes 68, 79–80
Owens, V.W. 13

PACTS (Parents and Children for Terrific
  Science) programme 19, 52
Paired Learning Project 59
Paired Maths
  in the classroom 71–82
  Diary/Record Cards 36, 39, 40, 41, 63
  educational practices related to 44–52
  evaluation of Kirklees projects 53–60
  evaluation methods 62–9
  materials for *see* games, mathematical
  organisation of 31–43
  rationale and development of 6–7, 8–9,
  9–10, 10–11, 14–17
  state of the art 90–91
Paired Reading 14, 21, 29, 32, 33, 37, 56,
  59, 64, 82
Paired Science
  Activity Sheets 18, 28, 29, 30, 34, 35, 36,
  39, 40, 41, 69
  evaluation methods 62–70
  materials for 20, 28–30, 34
  organisation of 31–43
  partners 34
  projects related to 44, 52
  rationale and development of 16,
  17–19
  research results 60–61
  state of the art 90–91
Parent Evaluation Questionnaire 42
Parent Resource in Support of Maths
  (PRISM) 13
'Parental Involvement in Science' pack
  19, 52
parents
  attitudes of 3–4, 37–8
  books for 105–7
  expectations of 5, 38
  involvement in maths 10, 12–14,

14–15, 21, 49–52, 53–4, 59, 63, 69
involvement in science 17, 18, 19, 52, 70
organising involvement of 31–43
Parents and Children for Terrific Science (PACTS) programme 19, 52
Parr, A. 45, 74
partners, 34
pattern 24, 25, 26, 86, 87, 95
peer partners 34
peer tutoring 12, 48–9, 71–82, 83–8
peer-assisted learning, value of 8–9, 10
Perry, J. 51
Phillips, N.B. 48
Piaget, J. 5–6, 18, 45
Pimm, D. 9
planning 31–6, 42–3
'Play Along Maths' programme 14
position 73, 74, 77
Pratt, S.J. 47
primary school children
    and cross-school peer tutoring 83–8
    and Paired Maths projects 55, 57, 71–82
PRISM (Parent Resource in Support of Maths) 13
probability 27
process evaluation 68, 76–8
puzzles 26, 27, 44, 73–4, 77, 80, 97–8

qualitative evaluation 57, 59, 62–4
quantitative evaluation 56–7, 57, 58, 64–8
QUEST diagnostic tests 56, 57, 58, 67
questionnaires 42, 62, 63, 64, 70, 76, 81

Raines, L. 2, 3
readiness 6
reading 14, 21 *see also* Paired Reading
Reciprocal Peer Tutoring (RPT) 48, 49
recruitment 33–5
Reid, J. 47
relations/relationships 26, 95, 97
Renwick 12, 49
Rillero, P. 19, 52

rods 23
Rogers, P.J. 45
rows 23
RPT (Reciprocal Peer Tutoring) 48, 49
rules for games 74, 76–7, 80

St Patrick's Primary School 84, 85
SAMI *(Sequential Assessment of Maths Inventories)* 68
school development plan 31
School Home Investigations in Primary Science (SHIPS) project 18, 19, 52
science
    cooperative learning in 11
    and the Internet 91
    language of 29, 38
    organising parental involvement in 31–43
    parental involvement in, 17, 18, 19, 52, 70
    peer tutoring in 12
    standards in 2–3, 17
    see also Paired Science
Science PACT 19, 52
Scotland 2–3, 12, 17–18, 48–9, 72 *see also* 5–14 Curriculum; UK/Britain
secondary sector 71–2
sequence 27
Sequential Assessment of Maths Inventories (SAMI; Reiseman) 68
severe learning difficulties, children with 46, 83–8
shape 24, 25, 26, 73, 74, 77, 86, 87, 96
shape, space and measures (curriculum) 24
Shaw Cross Project 60
SHIPS (School Home Investigations in Primary Science) project 18, 19, 52
Shire, B. 9
Simmons, K. 51
Singapore 2
Skemp, R.R. 7, 10, 20, 23, 28, 45, 57, 81
software, computer 91, 104
space games 26, 27, 96, 98–9

special needs 33, 83–8
'Staffordshire Mathematics Test' 66
stages of development 5–6, 7
Standardised Attainment Tasks 65
standards 2–3, 17–18
'Stanford Diagnostic Tests' 66
strategy 26, 27, 73, 74, 77, 86, 96, 98
Student Teams Achievement Divisions
  model 47
'Sums for Mums' project 13
Switzerland 2

Tangrams 23
teachers 15, 54, 59, 69, 79–80
'Test of Early Mathematics Ability'
  (TEMA-2) 66
'Test of Mathematical Abilities'
  (TOMA-2) 66
tests 54–5, 56, 57, 58, 64, 65, 66–8, 69,
  75–6, 79, 81
TIMMS (Third International Mathematics
  and Science Study) 2–3, 4, 17
training
  for peer tutoring 48
  teachers 15

UK/Britain 2–3, 11, 13–14, 47, 50–52
Urion, D.K. 47
USA 2, 4–5, 12, 13, 19, 52, 66, 68
  Department of Education 13, 91, 92
using and applying mathematics
  (curriculum) 24

video recording 77, 78
Vygotsky, L. S. 6, 7, 18

Wales 2 *see also* UK/Britain
Webb, N.M. 47
websites 91–2, 104–5
Whitebread, D. 7, 81
Wiliam, D. 4, 47, 65
women 1, 3, 13 *see also* gender; mothers
Wood, D. 47
Woolgar, J. 50

Young Mathematics group tests 54–5
Young Reading group tests 54–5